ESRI

THE ECONOMIC AND SOCIAL RESEARCH INSTITUTE

The Economic and Social Research Institute (ESRI) is a non-profit organisation which was founded in 1960 as The Economic Research Institute. The Institute is a private company, limited by guarantee, and enjoys full academic independence. It is governed by a Council consisting of 32 members who are representative of business, trade unions, government departments, state agencies, universities and other research institutes.

"GETTING OUT OF THE HOUSE"

Women Returning to Employment, Education and Training

Helen Russell, Emer Smyth,
Philip J. O'Connell and Maureen Lyons

The Liffey Press
in association with
The Economic and Social Research Institute

Published by
The Liffey Press
307 Clontarf Road
Dublin 3, Ireland
www.theliffeypress.com

A catalogue record of this book is
available from the British Library.

ISBN 1-904148-12-3

This study was commissioned by National Women's Council of
Ireland and the Department of Justice, Equality and Law Reform

Printed in the Republic of Ireland by Colour Books Ltd.

CONTENTS

FOREWORD

Gráinne Healy
Chairwoman, National Women's
Council of Ireland

The National Women's Council of Ireland welcomes the publication of this research by The Economic and Social Research Institute on women returners which will contribute to our understanding of the needs of women wishing to re-enter the workforce. It was estimated in 2000 that there were approximately 531,000 women on home duties in Ireland. While many of these women are not in a position to return to paid employment because of their caring responsibilities, a significant number of women do wish to return to the workforce. Are these women being supported to exercise their choice to re-enter paid employment? Are their particular needs and interests being addressed by current Government policy?

The National Women's Council of Ireland has long been conscious that the needs of women returners have not been accorded sufficient prominence by policy-makers. As many of these women remain outside existing support networks, their particular concerns can remain unknown and unaddressed. As the Technical Support Structure for the EU's New Opportunities for Women (NOW) Programme until 2000, the NWCI supported projects working with women returners. One of the key issues that emerged from the NOW Programme was the need for research to be undertaken which would ascertain the information and support needs of women returners. The NWCI approached the Department of Justice, Equality and Law Reform to obtain its support for research to be undertaken by the Economic and Social Research Institute and managed by the NWCI.

The ESRI's research examines both the particular needs of women returners and the barriers experienced by many women wishing to return to paid employment following a period engaged in caring work in the home. Using data generated by the Living in Ireland Surveys, supplemented by focus groups of key stakeholders (women returners, service providers, state agencies and key informants), the ESRI has developed an interesting picture of the experience of women returners trying to effect a transition from unpaid work in the home to education, training or paid employment.

The ESRI has highlighted a number of key issues in relation to women returners. Its findings indicate that more needs to be done to address the needs of these women so that they can enter secure, adequately paid and sustainable employment. What this research has found is that many women returners experience "downward mobility" when they return to the workforce, being forced into positions of lower socio-economic status than those they left to engage in full-time caring work. This research has also identified that many women returners work in low-paid jobs in catering, cleaning or childcare, areas which are an extension of the unpaid work undertaken by them in their homes.

As can be expected, the ESRI has found that the length of time spent out of the workforce is a key factor in determining a woman's success in returning to paid employment. The longer a woman spends out of the workforce, the weaker her chances of making a successful transition to paid employment. This finding highlights the particular supports required by older women returners who will often require skills upgrading to re-enter a workforce which has changed significantly over the past two decades.

The ESRI's research also draws attention to the continuing problem of childcare for most women with young children. Women with children under five, for instance, found that the absence of adequate childcare became a particular barrier preventing them returning to paid employment. While the Government has committed €435 million to increase the supply of childcare in the period to 2006 and has raised Child Benefit by €63 per month in the last two budgets, this research confirms the need for radical action to tackle a continuing crisis in childcare supply and to guarantee childcare places for all children whose parents wish to avail of such services.

What has also emerged in this research is the need for a significant improvement in the family-friendly policies offered by employers. Women speak in this research of how they were forced to give up work because their working conditions remained highly inflexible. Most women interviewed expressed an interest in part-time work so that they could combine their caring responsibilities with paid employment. There is an opportunity for the Government to take action to support employers to introduce more wide-ranging family-friendly policies such as paid parental leave. Irish employers can also learn more from the examples of good practice used by employers in other EU countries such as in Scandinavia, for instance, where the percentage of women in the workforce is the highest in the EU. Developing more flexible working conditions will increase the pool of those available for work and will draw on the significant expertise of women, often forced to withdraw permanently from the workforce due to the absence of childcare and family-friendly supports.

This research has identified lack of education as a particular barrier for a significant proportion of women returners. In general, women returners are educationally disadvantaged, having lower than average educational attainments. If women returners are to be enabled to exercise their right to return to paid employment, then the Government must recognise their educational needs and put in place programmes which can provide them with the education and skills necessary to enter sustainable employment. The *Report of the Partnership 2000 Working Group on Women's Access to Labour Market Opportunities* recommended that women returners should be given the right to access state educational and training programmes. Unfortunately, the recommendations of this report have not yet been fully implemented. FÁS needs to ensure, for instance, that all of its regional offices implement its stated commitment to open its training programmes to women returners, regardless of whether or not they are on the Live Register. The Department of Education and Science has yet to implement the recommendation to which it agreed in the report, namely that all women returners would have access to the VTOS scheme.

This research confirms the success of training programmes offered in accessible locations and at times which suit women with caring responsibilities. Both CERT and FÁS have introduced more flexible hours and locations on a limited range of courses; however, flexible provision needs to become more widespread. Community Education programmes offer a useful model in this respect. The childcare allowance introduced for participants on FÁS courses in 2001 is welcome — its effectiveness should usefully be reviewed at the end of 2002 to ensure that the criteria governing this allowance (such as that it is available only on a vouched basis) meet the needs of women who draw on informal family networks to meet their childcare requirements. Focus group participants identified a need for training courses in accessible locations, close to their homes. This finding confirms the need for state agencies and Government departments to support women's community education and training organisations which can potentially respond to a greater proportion of women returners' education and training needs.

In general, the continuing barriers experienced by women returners, coupled with the fact that many such women remain outside existing support networks, point to the need for the Government to implement the recommendation in the National

Economic and Social Forum's *Alleviating Labour Shortages* report (2000), namely that a National Support Programme for Women Returners should be established. The establishment of a national programme which would explicitly target women returners and respond to the diversity of their education, training and guidance needs becomes a priority when one considers the serious difficulties experienced by so many women returners in obtaining adequately paid employment. It is also important that the Government should develop an information campaign to make women returners aware of their existing entitlements.

The ESRI has undertaken an excellent piece of research which brings into focus the needs of an often-forgotten group. On behalf of the NWCI, I would like to thank Drs. Helen Russell, Philip O'Connell and Emer Smyth of the ESRI and Dr Maureen Lyons of the National Homeless Agency for their work in preparing a highly interesting publication which identifies the primary needs of women returners and the areas on which action must now be taken by the Government, state agencies, employers and key stakeholders. I would also like to thank the Department of Justice, Equality and Law Reform for its support in funding this research. I wish to express my gratitude to members of the Research Advisory Committee drawn from Government departments, state agencies and the social partners for their advice and support.

Gráinne Healy, Chairwoman
National Women's Council of Ireland
March 2002

ACKNOWLEDGEMENTS

This research was funded by the Department of Justice, Equality and Law Reform under the equality for women measure, and was administered by the National Women's Council of Ireland. We gratefully acknowledge the support of both bodies.

The research team has benefited greatly from the contributions of a wide number of people. First and foremost, we would like to thank the women returners, women in the home, and service providers who gave generously of their time and experiences in focus groups and interviews. The members of the steering group provided insightful comments on the work in progress and were very helpful in identifying contacts among service providers and in sourcing background information. Special thanks are due to the staff of the Department of Justice, Equality and Law Reform; Mary Beggan of FÁS and Tony Lenihan and Siobhan Lynch of CERT who contacted trainees on our behalf to participate in the research; Junette Dolan who helped us contact rural women; and Jacinta Donnelly who facilitated contact with the Rowlagh women's group. We are extremely grateful to Carol Baxter of the National Women's Council of Ireland who provided unstinting support to the research team throughout the project.

The analysis of the Living in Ireland survey data included in this report was made possible through the work of the survey unit in the ESRI, especially Dorothy Watson, and was hastened by programming work by Bertrand Maître, Brenda Gannon and Richard Layte. Jacqui Craig provided valuable and enthusiastic research assistance during her time at the ESRI. We would also like to thank ESRI colleagues who provided helpful comments on the initial draft of this report.

Responsibility for the contents of the report remains with the authors alone.

Helen Russell
Emer Smyth
Philip J. O'Connell
Maureen Lyons

LIST OF TABLES AND FIGURES

List of Tables

List of Figures

Chapter 1

INTRODUCTION

1.1 Background and Existing Research

The last decade has seen an unprecedented rise in labour force participation among Irish women and this has been an important factor behind the rapid economic growth that Ireland experienced during the 1990s. In 1990, just 35 per cent of women were active in the labour market but by the third quarter of 2001, this figure had risen to 50 per cent. Over the same time period, the number of women in employment rose by 349,000, which represents an increase of 89 per cent.[1] A significant part of this change has been fuelled by women moving from the home to employment. Therefore the story of Ireland's economic transformation rests in part upon the story of women returners. Yet relatively little attention has been paid to the process of returning to the labour market — such as the factors that spark the decision to return, the timing, the barriers, and the outcomes for those who attempt this transition.

Despite rising female participation, emerging labour shortages have prompted employers, politicians and policy makers to look at policies that might facilitate even more women to move back into the labour force.[2] While this may lead to positive changes in employment practice and has focused attention on

---

[1] These figures are taken from the QNHS and LFS reports published by the CSO.

[2] Within the context of labour shortages, NESF (2000, p. 96) recommended the establishment of "a National Support Programme for Women Returners to meet their specific needs".

important issues such as childcare, it is crucial that the views and needs of women themselves are taken into account and not simply the needs of the economy. It is important that women are not seen merely as a "reserve army of labour" to meet fluctuating demands and that support to return to the labour market or education is not contingent upon labour shortages. This study aims to investigate the experience of women returners in Ireland, focusing on returns not only to employment but also into education, training and employment schemes.

To date there has been a relatively small literature on the transition from full-time work in the home to employment or to education/training in Ireland. Mulvey's (1995) study of the transition to paid work in the Clondalkin area of Dublin found that the key barriers to work were lack of suitable childcare, lack of confidence and skills, lack of information and advice, and exclusion from the employment/training schemes because of Live Register requirements.

A report by the Employment Equality Agency (Cousins, 1996) addressed the more specific issue of women returners' access to training and employment schemes.[3] It focused on the exclusion of women returners from official definitions of unemployment and hence their exclusion from training or employment programmes with Live Register requirements. Cousins also concluded that the lack of clear, publicised eligibility criteria surrounding education, training and employment schemes led to widespread confusion. These issues were taken up again in *The Report of the Working Group on Women's Access to Labour Market Opportunities* (Department of Social, Community and Family Affairs, 2000). The report made a range of recommendations about extending programme access to returners, who they define as "returners/entrants to the labour force who have been primarily engaged in domestic and caring duties in the home, who are available for and genuinely seeking work". The working

---

[3] The study focuses on programmes run by FÁS, the Department of Education (e.g. VTOS), the Department of Social Welfare, Teagasc, and CERT.

group also highlighted the need for flexible provision of training and education and the need for adequate childcare provision.

A recent qualitative study outlined the difficulties faced by lone parents seeking to re-enter the labour market (Russell and Corcoran, 2000). This group found it extremely difficult to find work or training opportunities that were compatible with their caring responsibilities or that provided sufficient income to meet childcare costs and compensate for the loss of benefits. The loss of secondary social welfare payments such as rent supplement also prevented lone parents from taking up employment. Continued confusion about the entitlement to retain the medical card meant this still acted as a disincentive, and highlighted the need to provide clear and comprehensive information (ibid., pp. 21–2). Lone parents' participation in training or employment schemes was restricted because few courses were offered on a part-time basis or provided childcare, and those aged under 21 found themselves excluded from VTOS educational programmes because of age restrictions (ibid., p. 23). Only Community Employment (CE) schemes appeared to offer sufficient flexibility. However, few of the women had found jobs through CE schemes and they were often viewed as self-development programmes rather than as a direct route into the paid workforce.

There is a small body of research that addresses the effectiveness of different types of training among returners. Research by O'Connell and McGinnity (1997) has shown that returners are concentrated in the least successful active labour market programmes. However, while research on programme effectiveness shows that CE does little to enhance the employment prospects of men, there is evidence that it can improve women's subsequent employment chances (Denny, Harmon and O'Connell, 2000).

Research by Lyons (2000), which explores the training decision of women returners, found that women who had completed specific skills training or employment subsidy programmes (e.g. back to work allowance) were more likely to enter employment than those who participated in direct employment schemes (e.g.

CE). There was no difference in the probability of entering employment between participants in general training and participants in direct employment schemes.

The Irish literature to date has provided little evidence on the type of jobs the returners enter or the conditions they face when they return to work. However, research in the UK has shown that returners often experience downward mobility, reduced earnings and fewer promotion opportunities when they re-enter the job market (Joshi and Hinde, 1993; McRae, 1993). There is some evidence that occupational downgrading is linked to the lack of information about job opportunities and restricted job search networks among returners (Chaney, 1981).

1.2 Study Objectives

This brief overview of research highlights the need for further information on the experiences of women returners. This study has a number of key objectives:

- Firstly, to provide a profile of those who are potential returners to employment, training or education, and of those who manage to (re)enter these spheres;

- Secondly, to assess the needs and barriers of those in home duties who are trying to access work, education or training;

- Thirdly, to examine the existing service provision for returners and to identify gaps in that provision;

- Fourthly, to formally assess the factors associated with making a successful transition;

- Fifthly, to examine the types of jobs entered by women returners and their rewards and conditions;

- Finally, on the basis of this research, to make recommendations on the services and supports necessary for returners.

1.3 Methodology

This study combines both qualitative and quantitative research methods, using both surveys and focus groups. The survey data allow us to depict the overall pattern among women returners as a whole. In contrast, the composition of the focus groups is, by its nature, selective. However, focus group interviews allow us to capture women's own experiences and provide "insights into the sources of complex behaviours and motivations" (Morgan, 1996). The use of focus groups has the advantage of allowing us to capture the richness and variety of people's experiences through qualitative methods and to place this alongside representative questionnaire data from a much greater number and broader range of individuals. This means we can draw conclusions about the population of returners but at the same time reflect some of the flavour of women's lived experiences.

The quantitative analysis draws on six waves of the Living in Ireland Panel Surveys carried out between 1994 and 1999. The survey was initiated in 1994 when 4,048 households were sampled and 9,904 individuals within these households were interviewed. In each subsequent year an attempt is made to re-interview all panel members. Household moves, deaths and refusal to participate all lead to attrition in the sample over time. However, where possible, households that have moved are traced, respondents who set up new households are followed, and any new adult household members are interviewed. Details on the sample size and response rates for each year are included in Table 1.1 at the end of this chapter.

The Living in Ireland surveys collect detailed information on respondents' employment situation, family status, job search behaviour, income, psychological and physical wellbeing as well as many other socio-demographic variables. The major advantage of this data source for a study of women returners is the ability to follow women over time and trace changes in their employment status. In our transition analyses in Chapter 5, we identify women who are in home duties in one year (year 1) and examine their employment status when they are re-interviewed the following year (year 2). Therefore we look at transitions in five pairs of years: 1994 to 1995, 1995 to 1996, 1996 to 1997, 1997 to 1998 and 1998 to 1999. In Chapter 6, we look at the characteristics of the jobs the women occupy in year 2. Further detail on the variables in the questionnaires is provided in Chapters 2, 5 and 6.

The qualitative element of the research draws on a series of focus group discussions with three distinct groups:

- Recent participants in state-provided training or community education

- Women out of the labour force and not currently accessing state or voluntary services (and with no record of participation in state-provided training)

- Service providers and key informants.

Within these groups, an attempt was made to include a broad range of women in terms of age and family composition. One of the groups specifically targeted women residing in rural areas in order to cover needs and barriers that may be more pressing in non-urban areas.

We conducted two focus groups with each of the three groups outlined above. The trainee groups consisted of women returners who had completed courses with FÁS, CERT and Rowlagh women's group (a community education group). Members of the project advisory committee in FÁS and CERT kindly agreed to contact women in this category on our behalf. The agencies attempted to select women in a range of age groups insofar as it was possible within such a small sample. Contact details for women in the Rowlagh women's group were provided by the co-ordinator. Both the trainee focus groups were conducted in Dublin. Fifteen women participated in the groups — six in one and nine in the other — and both groups included a mix of women from the three programmes. While these focus groups provide useful insights into the process of finding out about, and taking part in, such programmes, it should be noted that the participants had all completed their courses and their views and experiences may differ to those of women who did not complete the courses or who did not agree to participate in the focus groups. Furthermore, the focus group participants from CERT and FÁS had all completed Return to Work programmes and so should not be taken to reflect the full range of courses entered by returners.[4]

The focus groups with women outside the labour market proved the most difficult to set up. An initial focus group was set up in Longford with the help of voluntary agencies in the area affiliated to the National Women's Council of Ireland (NWCI). This group was attended by ten women. During the focus group, it became apparent that many of the women had taken steps to re-enter the labour market. Some had taken training or education courses and others were involved in part-time work. Therefore only a subset of the group fitted our criteria of being totally outside the employment or training/educational spheres. Therefore a second focus group of four women was brought together in Dublin using personal contacts and snowball methods. The difficulty in identifying this target group highlights the blurring of boundaries between conventional labour market categories for women with caring responsibilities, as will be discussed in the next chapter. It may also reflect the fact that women working full-time in the home who are isolated from existing information networks will not be accessed easily for participation in studies of this kind. Participants in these two focus groups and the trainee focus groups were asked to complete a short questionnaire on their labour market experiences and family composition at the end of the discussion.

Finally, two focus groups were set up with service providers and key informants. These consisted of representatives of a range of organisations who have contact with or provide services for returners. The organisations involved included:

- Age and Opportunity
- Private training agency
- Chambers of Commerce of Ireland

---

[4] It was not possible to identify returners among participants on other courses.

- Clondalkin Women's Network
- Forfás
- Irish National Organisation for the Unemployed (INOU)
- Irish Farmers' Association (IFA)
- Irish Nurses' Organisation (INO)
- One Parent Exchange and Network (OPEN)
- Tesco Ireland.

Additionally, one-to-one interviews were conducted with representatives from FÁS and CERT, the Mature Students Officer in TCD and a VEC Adult Education Organiser.

The focus groups lasted about two hours on average, and were led by two or three facilitators. The focus group discussions were recorded using both video and audio tape. One of the facilitators operated a small digital camera on a tripod, with two microphones on stands. The tape recorder was used as a backup. The advantage of this method is that it solved the difficulty of deciphering who is speaking, it provided excellent sound quality and it removed the need for note-taking, thereby ensuring a free-flowing discussion. Although some of the participants were wary of the camera initially, once the discussion began they forgot it was there. All of the discussions were fully transcribed for the analyses.

1.4 Chapter Plan

This study is divided into six chapters. Chapter 2 clarifies our definition of potential returners and draws on analyses of the Living in Ireland Surveys to profile this group. Chapter 3 focuses on service provision for returners. Using information from service providers and secondary data sources, it describes the nature of this provision and perceived gaps. The chapter also includes women's experiences of service provision drawn from focus groups with women who have recently participated in training or education programmes. Chapter 4 again draws on the focus group material to explore the needs and barriers faced by women returning to work, education or training. Chapter 5 focuses on the factors that promote women's return to the workforce. We use the Living in Ireland panel survey data to explore the characteristics of women who make the transition from home duties into employment or education/training/employment schemes. In Chapter 6, we concentrate on women who have returned to employment and investigate the quality of the jobs they enter in terms of occupation, hours, pay and job satisfaction. The final chapter outlines the main conclusions of the study and highlights the policy implications of the research.

Table 1.1: Household and Individual Response Details, Living in Ireland Surveys 1994–1999

	1994	1995	1996	1997	1998	1999
Households						
Completed Households	4,048	3,584	3,174	2,945	2,729	2,378
Non-Response	3,038	794	624	390	391	464
Non-Sample	166	98	125	119	96	83
Total Households	7,252	4,476	3,923	3,454	3,216	2,925
Household Response Rate	57%	82%	84%	88%	87%	84%
Individuals						
No. in Completed Households	14,585	12,649	10,939	10,006	9,045	7,721
Eligible for Interview*	10,418	9,048	7,902	7,255	6,620	5,719
Completed Interviews	9,904	8,531	7,488	6,868	6,321	5,451
(% Completed)	95%	94%	95%	95%	96%	95%

* Aged 17 and over.

Chapter 2

PROFILE OF POTENTIAL RETURNERS

2.1 Introduction

In this study we define returners as women who have spent a period outside the labour market, in full-time caring or home duties, who (re)enter employment, education or training. This definition includes women who have never had a paid job before, but went straight from education to rearing their family. So some of the women will be entering the labour market for the first time rather than "returning". The defining factor is spending time full-time in the home before entering the labour market or education/training. By including education as a "return", we are moving away from conventional definitions which define education and training as non-participation. We also identify "potential returners", that is, women who are currently involved in home duties who have not yet made the transition back into work, education or training, but who might do so. It is this group of potential returners that we will follow over time, to see if they make a transition into one of these statuses.

Any attempt to classify women's labour market situation immediately runs into the problem that many of the labour market concepts and categories were developed to explain and describe male working patterns. For men, full-time continuous employment until retirement age has traditionally been the norm, and any break in employment is assumed to be involuntary. Therefore, distinguishing between employment, unemployment and economic inactivity among men is generally straightforward.[1] Women's participation in the labour market is much more variable over the life cycle. Transitions out of and back into the labour market around child-rearing, greater involvement in part-time employment, and ongoing responsibilities for domestic and caring work when in paid employment can all blur the boundaries between being outside the labour market (economic inactivity), employment and unemployment. Women's unpaid involvement in a family business or farm can also lead to an ambiguous labour market position, a point which was emphasised by agencies representing rural women and older women in the qualitative element of this research. The complexity of women's experiences of paid employment is often not adequately captured in the employment classification system. Therefore, women's labour market status is more accurately described as a continuum than a series of distinct statuses with rigid boundaries. At one end are those women who are completely outside the labour market and with no desire to return, and at the other are women in full-time, continuous employment. This continuum is represented in Figure 2.1. On the left side are the potential returners, i.e. women in home duties who are not involved in paid work, education or training, and on the right side are women who have taken a step into a range of activities.

As labour market attachment tends to change over the life cycle, women's position along this continuum is not fixed over time. Indeed, our attempts to identify a group of women outside the labour market for focus group discussions (described in Chapter 1) emphasised the fluidity in women's labour market status. While these women were initially thought to be outside the employment/education and training systems, after detailed discussions it was apparent that the women had a variety of attachments to informal and formal employment and to education/ training programmes. A further implication of the ambiguity in

---

[1] There is of course some ambiguity at the margins, for example in classifying discouraged workers and the early retired.

women's labour market status is that women's self-defined status may differ from administrative definitions (e.g. social welfare categories) and survey definitions (e.g. International Labour Office definitions). In section 2.4 below, we examine the overlap between our definition of women returners and official categories.

Figure 2.1: Continuum of Women's Involvement in the Labour Market

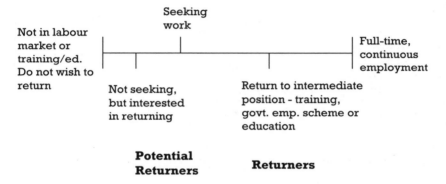

2.2 Number of Women in Full-time Home Duties

The figures included in Table 2.1 outline the number of women who are in full-time home duties in Ireland and so represents the potential pool of returners. These figures come from the Quarterly National Household Survey, so the age cut-offs and definition of home duties differ slightly from those used in the present study described below.[2] The figures show that the number of Irish women in full-time home duties dropped by over 50,000 between 1994 and 2000. Given that this change occurred in a period of population growth, the percentage decline was even more dramatic: in 1994, 43.4 per cent of Irish women were in full-

---

[2] These figures come from Table 20 of the QNHS reports. It counts women whose ILO status is "other" or "marginally attached to labour force" (i.e. not ILO employed or unemployed) and whose PES status is "Home Duties". The age range is 15-plus whereas our analysis is confined to those aged 17–65.

time home duties, but by 2000 this had fallen to 34.8 per cent. Despite this change, there are still over half a million women in home duties for whom the issues of access to employment, education and training opportunities may be relevant.

Table 2.1: Population Estimates of Women in Home Duties (all over 15 yrs)

	No.	% of Adult Women
1994	581,360	43.4
1995	574,271	42.3
1996	532,512	38.8
1997	547,423	39.2
1998	550,225	37.3
1999	533,807	35.6
2000	531,000	34.8

Source: LFS and QNHS

2.3 Identifying Potential Returners from the Living in Ireland Surveys

Within the general framework outlined above, we seek to identify women outside employment, training/education and to assess their level of attachment to the labour market. We begin with those who define their main activity as "home duties". On further investigation, some of these are found to be engaged in paid work (for less than 15 hours a week). Although these women primarily maintain a domestic identity, they have already made a transition into employment and so are further along the continuum than "potential returners".[3] We have applied an age cut-off of 65 years because research by Fahey and

---

[3] This definition of women in home duties differs from that used in Table 2.1 in that it includes women who are ILO unemployed, i.e. not in paid work, actively searching for work and available to start work, but who describe themselves as in home duties.

Russell (2001, p. 58) found that only a small minority of women aged over 65 have any interest in returning to employment. Including this group would have an unduly negative effect on the transition rates.

We also examined the characteristics of women who defined themselves as unemployed to see if any of these might be classified as potential returners. Taking the 1994 sample, we found that among this group nobody had left their last job for family reasons (marriage, children, caring duties) and many were first-time job seekers. In addition, none of this group reported spending any time in home duties, when they were asked to report how they had spent their time since leaving school. As there was no evidence of a "voluntary" interruption in employment for domestic reasons, we did not reclassify any of this group as returners.

The primary information that the Living in Ireland survey (LIS) contains on the labour market attachment of women in home duties is whether or not they are seeking employment. Respondents whose main activity was not work were asked: "Are you at present seeking work (either full-time or part-time) whether as an employee or self-employed?" Those seeking work are assumed to be further along the continuum towards employment than those who are not looking for work.

Table 2.2 contains information on the proportion of the women in home duties seeking work in each of the survey waves. There is no definite trend in the proportion of those in home duties seeking work; however, the low numbers seeking work in 1999 appears to be an outlier. This drop in job search in 1999 may have arisen because improved labour market circumstances meant that those who want employment will have already found it; this is more likely with panel data where we are interviewing many of the same people each year. As outlined above, the number of women in full-time home duties has been shrinking over time; however, they still represent a significant number in the population. The population figures suggest that in 1998 there were 24,147 women in the home looking for employment.

Table 2.2: Job Search Activity among Women in Home Duties (%)

	1994	1995	1996	1997	1998	1999
Seeking work	9.3	5.8	5.2	8.4	6.0	3.1
Not seeking	90.7	94.2	94.8	91.6	94.0	96.9
Total	100.0	100.0	100.0	100.0	100.0	100.0
Unweighted N	*2,352*	*1,993*	*1,707*	*1,490*	*1,350*	*1,145*
N pop weight	*472,466*	*448,274*	*419,602*	*423,331*	*402,442*	*360,192*

Note: the percentages reported in Tables 2.2 to 2.11 are based on weighted data and refer to women aged under 65 years.

2.4 Official Status of Women in Home Duties

From a policy perspective, it is of interest to establish the position of potential returners within the benefit system. For example, do any of the group appear on the official unemployment register, and are any of the group receiving other state benefits? The answers to these questions are important, as they shed light on the portion of the group who may have access to services and supports targeted at these different administrative categories.

There are three main administrative categories into which these women might fall. First, some may appear in the unemployment register and be in receipt of unemployment-related benefits. Second, some may be in receipt of lone parent benefits or another income support in their own right. Thirdly, they may be married to a man claiming a social welfare benefit or pension and so would appear in administrative records as a "qualified adult" for whom the claimant is paid an extra allowance.

The Living in Ireland surveys include questions on whether respondents are in receipt of various benefit payments. The majority of women in full-time home duties do not receive any of the social welfare payments outlined in Table 2.3: 72 per cent in 1994 and 70 per cent in 1998 received no benefits. The proportion of women in home duties receiving unemployment payments (Unemployment Benefit or Unemployment Assistance) and who therefore appear on the Live Register was 3.5 per cent in 1994 and 4.6 per cent in 1998. This estimate will exclude women who were not receiving unemployment payments but were registered to receive contribution credits.[4] However, even signing-on for credits is not an option for many women in home duties due to an absence from insurable employment of more than two years. Women in home duties seeking work were more likely to be on the Live Register; this association may arise because those receiving unemployment payments are required to actively seek work.

Table 2.3: Benefits Receipt among Women in Full-time Home Duties, 1994 and 1998 (%)

	Home Duties 1994			Home Duties 1998		
Current Benefits	*Seeking Work*	*Not Seeking*	*All*	*Seeking Work*	*Not Seeking*	*All*
None	62.6	72.6	71.7	64.8	70.1	69.8
Unemployment payments	8.8	2.9	3.5	18.1	3.7	4.6
Sick/Disability/ Injury	—	4.1	3.7	—	8.7	8.2
Survivors benefits	1.8	5.7	5.3	0.9	4.7	4.5
Lone Parents	24.0	9.9	11.2	14.1	8.8	9.1
FIS	—	0.8	0.8	—	1.3	1.3
SW schemes	2.9	3.8	3.7	2.1	2.3	2.3
Other	—	0.2	0.1	—	0.4	—
	100.0	100.0	100.0	100.0	100.0	100.0
Unweighted N	*137*	*1,660*	*1,797*	*40*	*876*	*916*

---

[4] In 1997, 13,791 women were signing on the Live Register for credits, which represented 5.3 per cent of all those on the register (Barrett et al., 2001, p. 16).

The most widely received benefits are those designed for lone parents;[5] 11 per cent of women in home duties were getting such benefits in 1994 and 9 per cent in 1998. Around 5 per cent of the group in both years were in receipt of survivor's benefits, e.g. widow's contributory or non-contributory pensions and survivor's benefit.

If women are not receiving benefits in their own right, they may be included in official records and be entitled to certain education programmes and employment schemes if their partner is claiming a state benefit and receiving a "qualified adult allowance". Women whose partners are not in receipt of state benefits do not have access to all such programmes and will not, therefore, be included in official records of this nature. In Table 2.4, we outline the employment status of the spouses/ partners of women in full-time home duties. We expect that those not at work will be in receipt of a state benefit of some kind. The "not at work" group includes those on state employment schemes because this group receive state transfers, which would include additions for qualified adults.

Table 2.4 shows that 27 per cent of women in home duties in 1994 could appear in government records as "qualified adults" because they have a partner who is not employed.[6] In 1998, the proportion is marginally lower at 25 per cent. In 1994, there is no difference in the percentage of job seekers and non-seekers who might be classified as qualified adults; however, in 1998, seekers appear less likely to fall into this category than non-seekers. Additionally, some of the "qualified adults" we identify might be claiming an insurance benefit in their own name or may be claiming a joint benefit (in families where both part-

---

[5] In 1994, the benefits included are Lone Parents Allowance or Deserted Wives benefit/allowance. In 1998 it included LPA, One Parent Family Payment, and Widowed Lone Parent Allowance.

[6] This measure of "qualified adults" is somewhat imperfect, as in a minority of cases the partner may not be in receipt of a social welfare payment. For example, a tiny number of husbands are in full-time education (two in 1994, none in 1998). However these cases are likely to be exceptional.

ners are unemployed, either person can claim the means-tested benefit).

Table 2.4: *Employment Status of Spouses/Partners of Women in Home Duties (%)*

	Home Duties 1994			Home Duties 1998		
	Seeking Work	*Not Seeking*	*All*	*Seeking Work*	*Not Seeking*	*All*
No partner[1]	28.0	19.7	20.5	14.8	17.8	17.6
Partner Emp.[2]	44.1	53.0	52.2	68.5	56.6	57.3
P not at work[2]	28.0	27.3	27.3	16.7	25.6	25.1
	100.0	100.0	100.0	100.0	100.0	100.0
Unweighted N	*137*	*1,660*	*1,797*	*40*	*876*	*916*

[1] Includes never married, separated, divorced and widowed.
[2] Partner includes spouses and cohabiting partners.

Due to the potential overlap between the two measures, in Table 2.5 we amalgamate the information on women's social welfare status. In both years, we find that just under half of the women in full-time home duties have some connection to the social welfare system. Between 3 and 5 per cent of the group appear on the Live Register and around a quarter of the group are in receipt of another income support benefit. The remaining 18–20 per cent are likely to be included as "qualified adults" in benefit records. In 1994, the proportion of women connected to the benefit system in some way is higher among those seeking work who are further along the participation continuum. In 1994, 73 per cent of those looking for work were either on the Live Register, in receipt of other benefits or were qualified adults. The figure in 1998 was 65 per cent.

Table 2.5: Claimant Status of Women in Home Duties, 1994 and 1998 (%)

	Home Duties 1994			Home Duties 1998		
	Seeking Work	*Not Seeking*	*All*	*Seeking Work*	*Not Seeking*	*All*
None	42.1	51.4	50.6	53.7	50.8	50.9
Reg. Unemp.	8.8	2.9	3.5	18.5	3.7	4.6
Other Benefit	28.7	24.4	24.8	16.7	26.2	25.7
Qualified adult[1]	20.5	21.3	21.2	11.1	19.3	18.8
	100.0	100.0	100.0	100.0	100.0	100.0
Unweighted N	*137*	*1,660*	*1,797*	*40*	*876*	*916*
Chi-square	*(p<.001)*			*(p<.001)*		

[1] Qualified adults are married women whose partners are not in employment; see text for further detail.

2.5 Characteristics of Women in Home Duties

In this section, we examine the characteristics of women in full-time home duties, who constitute the population of potential re-turners. We compare the characteristics of those who are seek-ing work with those of women who are not currently on the job market, which provides a profile of two groups at different points on the labour market continuum described above.

Focusing on the first wave and fifth wave interviews as ex-amples, we see that, in both years, women actively looking for work are younger than those not seeking work (see Figure 2.2). In 1994, the average age of seekers was five years lower than for non-seekers and in 1998 this had widened to a difference of nine years.

Figure 2.2: Mean Age of Women in Home Duties, 1994 and 1998 (Under 65s)

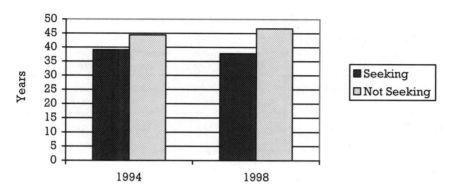

Previous work experience is likely to be a useful predictor of women's future attachment to the labour market. Studies of labour market entrants have also shown that work experience can increase the chances of finding employment (Russell and O'Connell, 2001). The great majority of women in home duties have some previous work experience (between 88 and 90 per cent). In both 1994 and 1998, seekers were more likely to have previous work experience than non-seekers (see Table 2.6).

We estimate the length of time out of the labour market using two measures. For women with work experience, we calculate the time that has elapsed since the last job. For women who have never been in paid employment we use the number of years they record in full-time home duties. In both years examined, we see that over a third (37–38 per cent) of women in home duties have spent more than 20 years out of the labour market; this is likely to have a significant impact on their possibility of entering employment and the support they would need to make such a transition. Those who have declared a current interest in returning (i.e. those seeking work) have spent a significantly shorter time outside the labour market than other women in home duties — see Table 2.7. In 1994, 41 per cent of seekers had spent less than five years out of the labour market compared to only 17 per cent of non-seekers. In 1998, the figures were 53 per cent and 21 per cent respectively, which suggests that the time that women are spending outside the labour market is declining.

Table 2.6: Previous Employment Experience among Women in Home Duties, 1994 and 1998 (%)

	1994			1998		
	Seeking	*Not Seeking*	*All*	*Seeking*	*Not Seeking*	*All*
Worked before	95.9	89.8	90.4	98.2	87.3	87.9
No prev. work	4.1	10.2	9.6	1.8	12.7	12.1
	100.0	100.0	100.0	100.0	100.0	100.0
Unweighted N	*137*	*1,660*	*1,797*	*40*	*876*	*916*
Chi-Square	(p<.01)			(p<.05)		

Table 2.7: Time out of Labour Force among Women in Full-time Home Duties (%)

	1994			1998		
	Seeking	*Not seeking*	*All*	*Seeking*	*Not seeking*	*All*
Less Than 2yrs	14.6	5.8	6.6	20.0	10.4	11.0
2–4.9yrs	26.3	11.0	12.5	32.7	10.3	11.6
5 to 9.9yrs	14.6	15.2	15.1	14.5	16.0	15.9
10–14.9yrs	17.5	14.6	14.9	9.1	11.9	11.8
15–20yrs	14.6	13.7	13.8	14.5	11.3	11.5
Over 20 yrs	12.3	39.7	37.1	9.1	40.0	38.1
	100.0	100.0	100.0	100.0	100.0	100.0
Unweighted N	*137*	*1,658*	*1,795*	*40*	*869*	*909*
Chi-Sq.	(p<.001)			(p<.001)		

Women in home duties have low levels of educational attainment compared to the general female population (Table 2.8).[7] Low educational levels among women in home duties is consistent with the finding that female labour market participation is very strongly linked to education in Ireland, especially among younger women (see Fahey et al., 2000). Thus it is mainly those with low education who remain in the home. There is no difference in the educational qualifications of seekers and non-seekers in either 1994 or 1998. However, if we collapse the categories further, we find a statistically significant relationship in 1998: seekers are more likely to have reached at least Leaving Certificate or above.

Table 2.8: Highest Education Qualifications of Women in Full-time Home Duties (%)

	1994			1998		
	Seeking	*Not seeking*	*All*	*Seeking*	*Not seeking*	*All*
No Quals	48.5	47.2	47.3	32.7	40.5	40.1
Inter Level	25.1	24.5	24.5	20.0	25.7	25.3
Leaving Level	20.5	24.0	23.7	43.6	28.5	29.4
Tertiary	5.8	4.4	4.5	3.6	5.3	5.2
	100.0	100.0	100.0	100.0	100.0	100.0
Unweighted N	*137*	*1,629*	*1,766*	*40*	*871*	*911*
Chi-square	*(n.s.)*			*(n.s.)*		

Another factor which may shed light on how close these two groups of women are to returning to the labour market is the degree to which they may be constrained by caring responsibilities. In general, women who are looking for work appear to face greater potential constraints than non-seekers. For exam-

---

[7] In 1998, 23 per cent of the women in the LII survey had no qualifications, 23 per cent had Intermediate Cert level, 38 per cent had Leaving Cert, and 17 per cent had third level qualifications.

ple, in 1994, 84 per cent of seekers had children under 18 compared to 69 per cent of non-seekers, which is consistent with the age difference between the two groups (Table 2.9). In both years, seekers are more likely to have responsibility for children under the age of 10 (not shown), and in the 1998 sample this group are also more likely to have children under the age of five (Table 2.10). However, in 1994, the non-seekers are marginally more likely to have a pre-school child (this difference is not statistically significant).

Table 2.9: Number of Children under 18, Women in Home Duties (%)

	1994			1998		
	Seeking	*Not Seeking*	*All*	*Seeking*	*Not Seeking*	*All*
None	13.5	30.5	28.9	10.9	38.6	37.0
One	30.4	19.0	20.0	30.9	21.6	22.2
Two	26.9	20.8	21.3	41.8	19.1	20.4
Three or more	29.2	29.8	29.7	16.4	20.7	20.4
	100.0	100.0	100.0	100.0	100.0	100.0
Unweighted N	*137*	*1,660*	*1,797*	*40*	*876*	*916*
Chi-square	(p<.001)			(p<.001)		

Table 2.10: Child Under the Age of Five, Women in Home Duties (%)

	1994			1998		
	Seeking	*Not seeking*	*All*	*Seeking*	*Not seeking*	*All*
No	76.7	70.6	71.2	52.7	77.2	75.8
Yes	23.3	29.4	28.8	47.3	22.8	24.2
	100.0	100.0	100.0	100.0	100.0	100.0
Unweighted N	*137*	*1,660*	*1,797*	*40*	*876*	*916*
Chi-square	(p<.001)			(p<.001)		

There is no difference in the incidence of elder care or caring for someone who is ill/disabled between the two groups of women in home duties (Table 2.11). These results suggest that caring responsibilities are not necessarily a good predictor of whether or not a woman is interested in returning to employment. Despite their more active stance in seeking work, job-seekers may face greater practical constraints in returning to work, education or training than those who are not currently looking to return. The multivariate models that we run in Chapter 5 examine whether caring responsibilities impact on women's success in re-entering the labour market, independent of age effects.

Table 2.11: Daily Activities Include Looking After Someone who is Elderly, Sick or Disabled: Women in Home Duties (%)

	1994			1998		
	Seeking	*Not seeking*	*All*	*Seeking*	*Not seeking*	*All*
Yes	10.5	12.5	12.3	7.3	9.7	9.6
No	89.5	87.5	87.7	92.7	90.3	90.4
	100.0	100.0	100.0	100.0	100.0	100.0
Unweighted N	*137*	*1,651*	*1,688*	*40*	*876*	*916*
Chi-square	(n.s.)			(n.s.)		

2.6 Multivariate Analysis

We have already seen that the tendency for women to seek to move from home duties into the labour market varies by a number of factors, including age, education and marital status. While this bivariate approach provides essential descriptive information about who is more likely to seek work, it does not allow us to assess the separate effects of different factors. For example, we cannot tell from these bivariate relationships whether the lower rates of seeking among older women is due to age *per se*, or to the differential distribution of recent work

experience across different age categories, or indeed to some
additional factor. In order to disentangle the separate effects of
a series of potentially influential factors, it is necessary to move
to a multivariate methodology within which we can control for
the effect of each variable when assessing the effect of another.

Table 2.12 shows a simple logistic regression model of the
probability of seeking work as a function of the characteristics
of individuals. The dependent variable in each of these equa-
tions is a dichotomous variable coded 1 if the respondent indicated that she was seeking work at the time of her interview,
and zero if she indicated that she was not searching.

**Table 2.12: Logistic Regression of Seeking Work among those
in Home Duties**

Variable	Coefficient	Std. Error
Intercept	−2.270***	0.408
Age < 25	Ref.	
Age 25–34	−0.409	0.290
Age 34–44	−0.551	0.317
Age 45–54	−1.046**	0.352
Age 55+	−1.815***	0.397
No Qualification	Ref.	
Junior Certificate	−0.088	0.142
Leaving Certificate	−0.515**	0.162
Tertiary	−0.229	0.271
1994	Ref.	
1995	−0.300*	0.153
1996	−0.610***	0.176
1997	−0.355*	0.172
1998	−0.592**	0.199
Married/with partner	Ref.	
Separated, Divorced or Widowed	−0.553	0.412
Never Married	−1.085*	0.453

Table 2.12 continued

Variable	Coefficient	Std. Error
No children under age 12	*Ref.*	
Youngest child under 5 years	−1.018***	0.209
Youngest child aged 5–12 years	0.329*	0.163
Partner working	−0.208	0.144
Caring	−0.167	0.189
Never worked	*Ref.*	
< 2 yrs since last job	2.126***	0.289
2–5 yrs since last job	1.682***	0.288
5–10 yrs since last job	1.060***	0.292
10–15 yrs since last job	0.905**	0.289
15–20 yrs since last job	0.795**	0.292
> 20 yrs since last job	0.306	0.276
Years working	0.406	0.369
Educ/Train, last year	0.878***	0.217
No SW Benefits	*Ref.*	
Pension	−3.346	10.113
Unemployment	0.995***	0.217
Sickness/Disability	−2.173**	0.719
Survivor	0.488	0.544
Lone Parent	1.231**	0.422
Family Income Suppl.	−1.677	1.025
SW Scheme	−0.071	0.308
Small town or rural	*Ref.*	
City	−0.066	0.123
N of cases	*5886*	
−2 log likelihood (intercept only)	*2804.73*	
−2 log likelihood (final)	*2391.30*	
Nagelkerke R^2	*0.177*	
* p < .05; ** p < .01; *** p < .001		

The data consist of cross-sectional information for each individual pooled over each of the five interviews from 1994 to 1998. Any individual will be present in any year that she participated in the survey and was engaged in home duties at the time of the interview. So a maximum of five observations can be taken of any individual, and we specify control variables for each of the years between 1994 and 1998 to take account of the fact that individuals are observed over a series of years. The model includes a large number of factors which could influence whether someone engaged in home duties would be searching for work. These include age, education, marital status and ages of youngest children, caring for elderly or other relatives, partner's employment status, previous labour market experience, receipt of social welfare income maintenance payments and urban residential location. Estimating a multivariate model allows us to assess the influence of each of these variables while taking account of the influence of the other variables in the model.

The model shows that women in home duties were more likely to be seeking work in 1994, the reference year, than in any other year in the period covered, and they were significantly less likely to be searching in 1995, 1996, 1997 and 1998. This negative effect of time on job search may be due to a type of selection effect, i.e. as labour market conditions improved over time, the duration of job search would decline; therefore job seekers would be less likely to appear in the sample. The years 1993 to 1998 were a period of exceptionally rapid growth in employment, particularly among women: total women's employment grew by over 6 per cent *per annum* between 1993 and 1998. With booming demand, particularly after 1994, this meant that the duration of the average woman's job search was likely to be relatively short, with the result that *on average* the probability of an individual being captured by the LIS sample was lower in the years following 1994.

Compared to women in the 16–25 year age group, the reference category, women aged over 45 years of age were significantly less likely to be searching for work, and the size of the effect increased with age group. When the effects of the other variables in the model are controlled for, attainment of a Leaving Certificate level of education had a negative impact on job searching, but no other educational variable differed from the reference category, those with no qualifications. This negative effect of Leaving Certificate attainment is also probably due to a selection effect whereby women at this level of education may be more likely to be already participating in the workforce, rather than to be in home duties, or, if searching, to be more likely to secure a job more rapidly than those with lower qualifications. In either case, they would have been selected out of the sample.

Never-married women who were engaged in home duties were somewhat less likely than those who were married or living with a partner to be searching for work. However, caring for elderly or other family members did not influence job seeking; neither did partner's current employment situation. The equation shows the effect of a partner working, but in other specifications of this model the effects of a partner being unemployed also showed no significant effect on respondents' job search.

The presence of children did influence job search. Women with youngest children under the age of 5 were substantially less likely than those with no children under the age of 12 to be searching for work. However, women whose youngest children were aged between 5 and 12 were more likely to be seeking work, compared to those in home duties with no children under age 12. The greater propensity of women with children in the 5–12 age group to search for work may appear counter-intuitive. However, this may be due to selection effects, whereby those women engaged in home duties with either no or older children may have a lower disposition to engage in paid work outside the home — many of those with a greater such disposition would have already accomplished the transition to work, and would therefore be excluded from the analysis.

Labour market variables are also influential. Recent work experience had a strong positive effect on job seeking: those who had any experience of working in the past 20 years were more likely to be seeking work than those who had never worked, the reference category, and the effect was strongest among those who had been at work within the previous two years. There was no difference, however, between those who had worked 20 or more years previously and those who had never worked. When time since the last job is taken account of, "years worked" expressed as a proportion of total years elapsed since age ten had no further impact on job seeking. Those who had participated in education or training in the past year were more likely to be seeking work.

Social welfare income maintenance was also related to job seeking. Recipients of unemployment payments and Lone Parent's allowance were more likely to be seeking work than the reference category of those who were not in receipt of any social welfare payments, while those receiving payments in respect of sickness or disability were less likely to be seeking work.

Urban/rural location had no impact on job seeking. Here, in addition to the specification of cities reported in Table 2.12, which includes residents of all urban areas larger than Waterford, we also investigated the effects of living in smaller urban centres, compared with open country, but found no significant differences.

We can summarise the model as follows. Older women engaged in home duties are less likely to be seeking work, as are those with a Leaving Certificate. When labour market variables are controlled for, women engaged in home duties who had never married are somewhat less likely than those with partners to be seeking work. Also, when labour market variables are controlled for, women with youngest children under age five were less likely to be seeking work, while those with children aged 5–12 were more likely to be seeking. Recent work experience, particularly in the past five years or so, has a positive effect on job search, as does recent participation in education or training. Receipt of certain social welfare benefits also influences job search: unemployment and lone parent's payments positively so, sickness and disability-related payments, negatively so.

2.6 Conclusions

In this chapter, we outlined the definition of returners used in this study. It was argued that women can often straddle a number of different labour market categories; for example, working part-time while still defining oneself as a housewife. Therefore it was suggested that women's attachment to the labour market might better be viewed as a continuum rather than a series of discrete categories. On one side of the continuum, we have women who are in full-time home duties who are not doing any paid work. We consider all of this group to be potential returners. This is a very sizeable group in the population, although their numbers are declining as more and more women participate in the labour market. Within this group, there will be women who are more or less interested in returning to the labour market — we use "seeking work" to distinguish these groups (unfortunately, there is no measure of interest in pursuing education options).

The analysis showed that, on average, 6 per cent of those in home duties were looking for work in each year. Those who declared themselves to be in the job market were significantly younger, and more likely to have recent work experience, than those who were not looking for work. Those in receipt of lone parent benefits and unemployment benefit or assistance were more likely to be seeking work than those receiving no benefits. The higher incidence of looking for employment among those on UA and UB may reflect administrative requirements to actively seek work; however, no such requirement is made of those claiming lone parent's benefits. Therefore, on face value, the benefit itself does not discourage participation in the labour market. The model showed that, when all years were pooled and other factors controlled, women in home duties with children under 5 were less likely to be looking for work than those with no children under age 12, whereas those with children aged between 5 and 12 were more likely to be on the job market. This is consistent with the qualitative data that we present below, which suggest that women commonly plan to re-enter the labour force when their children are in primary school.

The absence of influence of a partner's employment status on women's job search is of interest, as it is often posited that male unemployment will discourage wives from participating in the labour market both because of the threat to benefit income and the challenge to traditional gender roles within the household. The current evidence suggests that this is not a barrier to job search; however, in Chapter 5, we will investigate whether it influences the take-up of employment.

Our models have shown in detail which type of individuals within the wider group of women in home duties are most likely to be looking for work. However, our discussion on the fluidity in women's labour market status should caution us against assuming that this desire for employment will necessarily remain stable for the period between interviews. Furthermore, there is evidence that women returners are often reluctant to declare that they are searching for work, but may nevertheless grasp employment opportunities when they are presented to them. Chaney's (1981) study of female returners in the UK found that 21 per cent of the women reported that they had "done nothing" to find their current jobs, yet some did not count perfectly legitimate forms of job search because they did not view themselves as unemployed (see also Martin and Roberts, 1984). Similarly, a British study of unemployed women including returners found that those who were not searching in 1986 were just as likely as active seekers to have found employment in 1987 (Russell, 1996, p. 177). Therefore we might expect that some of those in the "not seeking" group will have made the transition into employment or education/training when they are re-interviewed a year later. This issue is returned to in Chapter 5.

Chapter 3

SERVICE PROVISION AND WOMEN RETURNERS

Two focus groups were conducted with representatives from key organisations providing services to, or having contact with, women returners. The organisations involved included:

- Age and Opportunity
- Chambers of Commerce of Ireland
- Clondalkin Women's Network
- Forfás
- Irish National Organisation of the Unemployed (INOU)
- Irish Farmers' Association (IFA)
- Irish Nurses' Organisation (INO)
- One Parent Exchange and Network (OPEN)
- A private training organisation
- Tesco Ireland.

In addition, individual interviews were carried out with representatives from CERT, FÁS, City of Dublin VEC and Trinity College Dublin.

This chapter describes the kinds of services provided by the groups included in the study along with the perceptions of education/training provision among those who have used such services.

3.1 Type of Services

The service providers included in the study differed in the extent to which they had direct contact with women returners and varied in the types of services they provided. Six of the organisations were involved in the direct provision of education/ training (among other services) to women returners while five of the groups adopted an advisory and/or lobbying role in relation to policy and provision.

Education and Training

Training courses for women returners are provided by FÁS and CERT while women returners also take part in education courses run by the VEC, community education groups and third-level institutions.

FÁS is described as being involved in the provision of guidance and counselling along with training courses:

> The first service is they have a guidance and counselling service available to them, so they can walk through the door and register with FÁS and they have a guidance and counselling service. And then they have a pool of jobs to look at if they want to go into work. (FÁS representative)

The main courses taken by women returners were described as return to work courses, computer-based specific skills training and enterprise training. In addition, women returners often attend courses provided by statutory agencies within the local community:

> We have community-based courses that aren't called return to work courses but they are return to work courses and they're geared to women but they are at the request of the community and they are done in conjunction or in partnership with the community groups and women's groups at community level. (FÁS representative)

These community-based courses were seen as providing flexibility in terms of the hours during which courses were run as well as overcoming potential transport problems for more geographically isolated groups.

FÁS training centres vary in terms of childcare provision for course participants. However, childcare allowances have been introduced from September 2001 for course participants on a "pay the provider" basis.

In 2000, 1,306 people took part in FÁS return to work courses, of whom 94 per cent were women (FÁS statistics, 2001; see Appendix 3.1 of this chapter). Return to work (RTW) courses combine an emphasis on skill development with confidence-building for those who have been out of the labour force for a number of years. RTW is a foundation-level course; the content varies from centre to centre but most courses include an emphasis on basic computing skills, job-seeking skills and personal effectiveness. Some of the RTW courses include a work placement. These courses vary in duration but normally last between 12 and 20 weeks. RTW courses are run on a part-time basis in some centres but are full-time in others. This variability in provision may allow for greater flexibility; however, variation in the criteria for course entry from centre to centre could lead to unequal access.[1] The precise number of women returners on other FÁS courses cannot be distinguished, although the overall proportion who are female varies across course types (DSCFA, 2000).

CERT runs some courses which "are not specifically for women returners" but are accessed by this group:

> We do elementary training in CERT House, and we have two out-reach centres in Ballymun [and] Clondalkin as well. That's elementary training in cookery, catering assistant skills, bar skills, reception, areas like that. . . . We

---

[1] Information on the FÁS website (www.fas.ie/servlet/) on RTW courses shows some have a requirement that participants are aged 25 and over (FÁS Cabra), others specify minimum education requirements (FÁS Athlone), while others state that "priority will be given to those on the live register" (FÁS Loughlinstown) even though few returners are on the register.

also have return to work courses, which are short 10-week, 100-hour courses, which are run all over the country. (CERT representative)

The elementary training courses are provided on a full-time basis while the return to work courses are provided on a part-time basis:

It could be two five-hour days, in the evening or in the daytime, whichever suits. (CERT representative)

The outreach centres have been developed in response to local demand:

It would tend to be the community groups who make contact with us and say, "Listen, I have a group of 10 people who would like to do a return to work, can you do it for us?" And they tend to be return to work women. (CERT representative)

In addition, courses are provided in temporary centres at different sites around the country in order to improve accessibility:

We do have temporary centres that open . . . in the winter which do elementary courses. They're normally based in hotels that close for the winter, so we move in. (CERT representative)

Childcare provision is dependent on the centre attended:

We don't provide it here [CERT House] because there are so many, there are 180 students here at any one time. It would be impossible (a) to find places for them, childcare, and (b) to fund it. But we do in the two centres out in Ballymun and Clondalkin. (CERT representative)

However, provision in the outreach centres is currently limited:

We have a limit on it. . . . We can pay for four places only per centre. . . . [But] then the local employment service

would top up if there's other people apart from those four
who need it. . . . (CERT representative)

Women returners are incorporated into general schemes provided by the City of Dublin VEC, such as the Vocational Training and Opportunities Scheme (VTOS),[2] the literacy scheme
and community education:

> There's a lot of centres around the city now where VEC
> would provide the hours, the tutors, and the centres
> themselves then put on the classes. And a lot of women
> come back through that. (CDVEC representative)

The CDVEC is involved in outreach activities:

> There is more emphasis now on advertising. We have lit-
> eracy outreach workers employed now that we never
> had before. So there would be four of those at the mo-
> ment. And even within the schemes there would be some
> of the tutors now who would be coming on, experienced
> tutors, and they would maybe do some outreach as part
> of their role. (CDVEC representative)

In addition, a pilot scheme on adult guidance is currently being
carried out:

> That came from a partnership between the VEC, Dublin
> Adult Learning Centre and the Dublin Inner City Partner-
> ship. . . . Because the Partnership were highlighting the
> fact that people weren't progressing either and moving
> on. So this was to sort of try and assist in that, people who
> were already in basic education can get advice and
> guidance about how to move on and encouragement in
> study support and so on. . . . It's focused on students who
> would be already in or maybe just coming into literacy
> schemes, students who would be in community education
> centres. (CDVEC representative)

---

[2] However, only women returners in social welfare-dependent households
can currently access VTOS provision.

The VEC provides a childcare allowance for VTOS participants and some centres have crèche facilities:

> In VTOS now there is a £50 childcare allowance per child and that helps. . . . Where the VEC can it has been providing its own crèches, say within the schools. [It] depends on what the local situation is. It might buy places in a community crèche once that's good quality care, and otherwise it maybe goes into partnership in building crèches or it has a crèche within the school. (CDVEC representative)

No figures are available on overall participation in adult education provision. In 2000, it is estimated that 14,591 adults took part in the adult literacy scheme. Sixty-four per cent of the participants were women and over one-quarter were not in the labour force (Department of Education and Science website, 2001).

Community education consists of adult education located physically within the community. Community education tends to differ from formal education in terms of course content, the learning process and modes of assessment employed (Department of Education and Science, 2000). It is estimated that there are around 1,000 women's community education groups with participation levels ranging from 30,000 to 100,000 nationally (WERRC, 2001). These groups are generally grassroots initiatives:

> A lot of the groups would have started from women living in isolation, not knowing their next-door neighbours, coming out to the schools, the social element around leaving the children into school. A lot of them would have stemmed out of maybe one or two religious sisters in the community or maybe the home–school liaison [officer] might have brought the women together to do maybe one course around parenting. From that once the women got a taste of it, [they] decided right, we're not going back here, we're going to continue. (Clondalkin Women's Network representative)

While the initial impetus for establishing such groups was not related to the labour market, groups have often acted as a mechanism for women to re-enter paid employment:

> A lot of the women that get involved initially in community education don't get involved to get a job. They get involved because they are living in isolation. . . . What happens within the women's groups in community education is that a progression route [evolves] . . . and without even knowing it, women are actually going through this progression route and at the end of that, it comes down to their choice, whether they do want to move into employment or whether they want to continue to do their education or go onto third-level. (Clondalkin Women's Network representative)

Although childcare provision is available in many of the groups, the number of places tends to be limited due to lack of resources.

Women returners may also access mainstream third-level education. However, in comparison with other European countries, the proportion of adults entering third-level education is low (Department of Education and Science, 2000) and the existence of specific measures to target adult entrants varies across institutions. Trinity College Dublin has a full-time Mature Students Officer and an access course for mature students. In addition, it offers a counselling service and learning support for mature entrants:

> The other support service is an extensive counselling service. And that is taken in its broadest sense, one-to-one, study skills. . . . Another one is immediate access to tutorials or grinds. . . . Say in the maths, they haven't done maths in ten years and they find that difficult. . . . I found that if I had a small fund and they come in and they say they need help, it's usually only three or four hours, I would say, "right, here is the money and here is a list of tutors", and those three or four hours intervention can be

amazingly effective. They work on elements, they give the person a chance to talk about their own difficulties, which is often to do with lack of confidence. And in a one-to-one, or one-to-two situation that is much more effective. (Mature Students' Officer, TCD)

TCD has a crèche but it "usually has a long waiting list". Overall, less than a third of all educational institutions provide childcare facilities for students and fewer than a quarter of those that do provide facilities can guarantee a place for the pre-school children of students (Higher Education Equality Unit, 1999).

Advice and Lobbying

A number of the service providers interviewed had an advisory or lobbying role which encompassed, but was by no means exclusive to, women returners. A representative from the INOU stated:

Primarily our role in relation to that group [women returners] is like it is in relation to the unemployed. It's campaigning for services.

The One Parent Exchange and Network plays a similar role on behalf of lone parents:

Our network . . . is an anti-poverty network so our membership would be made up mostly of lone parents who are in receipt of social welfare payments. . . . We provide information, training and support to our member groups and it's groups as opposed to individual lone parent support. And then . . . we are a lobbying organisation to government . . . we're the only lone parent organisation involved in social partnership. (OPEN representative)

Age and Opportunity is, as the name suggests, concerned with the needs of older people:

Age and Opportunity is not a service provision organisation, it's about attitudinal change and it's about people valuing older people for the contribution that they make and for older people themselves seeing that what they have to offer has a value. . . . It's about changing the way people look on older people. (Age and Opportunity representative)

In addition, the Chambers of Commerce of Ireland plays an advisory role in relation to employers:

We have been campaigning on facilitating the return to work of women and that would be particularly focusing on campaigning for childcare. (CCI representative)

3.2 Profile of Client Group

Service providers were questioned about the kinds of women returners who made contact with their organisation. A number of service providers considered that women returners tend to fall into two categories: firstly, women with older children who may have been some time out of the labour market; and secondly, younger women with young children, a group frequently but not exclusively made up of lone parents:

They [returners] would fall broadly into two camps. . . . You see women in their twenties who became parents, probably lone parents, at a relatively young age . . . and who had been out of the workforce for a couple of years and who were looking to get back. And for some of those groups, their previous labour market attachment would have been pretty weak, it would have been low-skilled jobs and none of them very permanent. And then the other category would be your older women who have essentially raised a child or a family and are the partners of unemployed men or the partners of low income men. (INOU representative)

What we have are ladies returning to work who have never worked before at all or the lone parent group who still have their children at home. (CERT representative)

> I suppose broadly there are two groups . . . one is women who leave the labour force more on a short-term basis, they might leave for . . . less than five years while their children are still small and they have to get back into the labour force again to pay for their mortgage or whatever. And then there's also a group of older women who've been out quite a long time. (Chambers of Commerce representative)

One organisation, Age and Opportunity, had contact with an older group of women:

> They are the women who had big families, by and large, many of them are the women who had to leave work because of the marriage bar. (Age and Opportunity representative)

Some of the service providers felt that the profile and motivations of returners had changed over time:

> The age group had dropped, they were coming back much quicker after having their children, they weren't taking that big time out, they wanted money towards the mortgage, they wanted an independent life, whereas the average away [from the labour force] would have been sixteen to eighteen years when we started out [with return to work courses] at first. (Private trainer)

> Up until a couple of years ago I would have said it was mainly younger women, women with children or women maybe with children just grown up, coming back into education for their own sakes. Then there has been a change in recent years, a lot more women coming back . . . thinking of work as well as education for its own sake. (CDVEC representative)

While varying somewhat in their composition, there was a view that those with lower educational qualifications were over-represented among women returners:

> I'd say they probably just got straight into having children and never went to work and just got married and had children, raised them, and probably had no education at all. . . . Literacy skills are a big problem, for the Return to Work [course] ladies in particular, because they never got schooling, a lot of them don't have the literacy skills either or the numeracy skills. (CERT representative)

> Everybody who attends the access course would have been early school leavers. . . . They would generally be in a group that wouldn't be educationally advantaged. (Mature Students' Officer, TCD)

It was stressed, however, that women returners represent a diverse group with consequent implications for devising appropriate provision:

> I think there is a problem with looking at all women who have been in the labour market at one stage and who are now coming back to it having the same set of needs. (Private trainer)

> Some women might need only a two-week course to refresh their skills while others might need much more intensive training; some might have literacy problems. (FÁS representative)

Furthermore, it was felt that the boundaries were often blurred between being "out" of the labour force and "returning":

> Women working in family businesses, and particularly farms, who are now twenty years down the line, who still don't exist and they are considered to have significantly contributed to the economic output on farms but nobody can find them anywhere and they're not going to get any benefit from it. . . . It's a grey area. (IFA representative)

The profile of women returners nationally has been outlined in the previous chapter. However, it is very difficult to determine

the profile of women returners accessing services on the basis
of existing statistics. Information is available on those women
coming through return to work courses but not through general
statutory or community-based provision. Over half of those taking FÁS return to work courses are over 45 years of age, the
majority (71 per cent) had not previously been in receipt of social welfare payments and a third had a Leaving Certificate
education (FÁS statistics, 2001; see Appendix 3.1). Among
those taking CERT return to work courses, a fifth have Leaving
Certificate qualifications while over a third have no formal
qualifications (CERT statistics, 2001).

3.3 Perceptions of Education and Training

It was beyond the parameters of the study to explore perceptions of all the organisations providing services to women returners. However, detailed focus group interviews with women
who had taken part in education and training courses yielded a
good deal of insight into their perspective on existing provision.

The women in this study were involved in training supplied
by FÁS and CERT and further education through a local Women's
Group. Within these categories the diversity of courses was
fairly significant. On the one hand, there were introductory arts
and crafts and personal development courses. On the other
hand, under the training umbrella, were courses that trained
people for semi-skilled and white-collar jobs. These included
courses in catering, book-keeping and computing.

The vast majority of women expressed a high level of satisfaction with their experience of adult training or education. In
fact, most expressed the view that the experience of training
made a substantial and positive difference to their lives. Personal gains mentioned included the ability to think differently
about their lives, increased motivation and the satisfaction of
having achieved something worthwhile. However, the benefit
that was most often stressed by the women was that education/
training gave them confidence in themselves. This was a key
factor, particularly for women whose daily lives had for many

years been spent at home with children or working in unskilled (predominantly cleaning) jobs. The following quotations illustrate the way that many of the women felt:

> The course involved all sorts of confidence building which was very good. Because of my experience of it I have now done a lot of personal work. It benefited me greatly. A lot of women who were doing the course were very lacking in self-confidence and the STEPS [personal development] programme was wonderful in helping with that. Everyone benefited from that. (FÁS course participant)

> The FÁS course gave me the wherewithal to move on. I couldn't have done it, I honestly couldn't have done it without the energy of that woman [trainer]. She was brilliant. (FÁS course participant)

> If it was not for FÁS I wouldn't be where I am today. I'd be inside in the hospital or somewhere. So it is very important for women in my age group (over 55) to get the confidence and also to have the support of the young girls. (FÁS and CERT course participant)

> On the second chance programme they build you up and I rediscovered things about myself that I'd left behind at school. You know, that I was actually good at writing, I had a quick mind and I could communicate. That was great. It made me decide never to do a cleaning job again. (Community education course participant)

> Our course was fantastic. We did computers, we did interview skills, we did trial application forms, we did mock interviews, safety and customer relations. (FÁS course participant)

> It was a way to make you think in a lateral way than, you know, at home, you just think in a narrow way. Whereas this made you think more laterally. By using these fun exercises, it was all pure fun. All in a fun way, all *craic*, you know. (FÁS course participant)

For these women, the training experience was undoubtedly a life-changing experience. However, a minority of women were critical that the content of the course was not what they were told it was going to be and were not satisfied with the quality of the instruction. It should also be noted that the perceptions of women who had dropped out of these courses before completion may differ from the views reported here.

3.4 Conclusions

This chapter has outlined the kinds of services potentially available to women returners, including education and training, along with advice and information. Education and training courses tend to vary in the hours during which they are run, whether they provide childcare for participants, and in the type of course provided. Among those women interviewed who had taken part in education/training, the vast majority were positive about their experiences, highlighting in particular the contribution to their self-confidence. However, not all potential returners currently access services. The extent to which barriers exist in accessing these services is discussed in the following chapter.

Appendix 3.1

Table 3.1: Gender Profile of Participants in FÁS Return to Work Courses, 2000

Gender	N	%
Women	1,225	93.8
Men	81	6.2
Total	1,306	100.0

Table 3.2: Age Profile of Female Participants in FÁS RTW Courses, 2000

Age Group	N	%
Under 25	23	1.9
26–35	109	8.9
36–45	423	34.5
46 plus	670	54.7
Total	1,225	100.0

Table 3.3: Educational Profile of Female Participants in FÁS RTW Courses, 2000

	N	%
None	197	16.1
Primary	178	14.5
Inter/Group/Junior	357	29.1
Leaving Cert	426	34.8
Higher	1	0.1
Other	66	5.4
Total	1,225	100.0

Table 3.4: Benefit Status of Female Participants in FÁS RTW Courses, 2000

	N	%
None	871	71.1
Credit	70	5.7
Disability Benefit	17	1.4
Lone Parent	13	1.1
Unemployment Assistance	96	7.8
Unemployment Benefit	102	8.3
Other Benefit	56	4.6
Total	1,225	100.0

Source: FÁS, European Finance Unit, special tabulations.

Table 3.5: Age Profile of Participants on Selected CERT Return to Work Courses (all female)

Age	N	%
18–21yrs	1	1.5
22–24yrs	4	6.2
Over 25	60	92.3
Total	65	100.0

Table 3.6: Educational Profile of Participants on Selected CERT Return to Work Courses

Education	N	%
No qualifications	23	35.4
Junior Cert	7	10.8
Inter Cert	19	29.2
Leaving Cert	14	21.5
3rd level	2	3.1
Total	65	100.0

Source: CERT, special tabulations.

Chapter 4

THE NEEDS OF WOMEN RETURNERS AND BARRIERS TO WORKFORCE RE-ENTRY

4.1 Introduction

This chapter draws on group interviews with women and service providers to examine the needs of women returners and perceived barriers to their successful re-integration into the labour market. Focus group interviews were conducted with six groups: two groups made up of representatives from key organisations providing services to, or having contact with, women returners; two groups of women who had recently completed an education or training course; a group of women living in a rural area who varied in their attachment to the labour market; and a group of women who were working full-time in the home. This chapter explores the common themes which emerged from these interviews.

4.2 Labour Force Withdrawal and Re-entry

The women in the focus groups were not a homogenous group but differed in terms of their own age, the age of their children, their family status and economic status of the household, their education and previous work history.

Among the women who had taken part in education/training, three-fifths had withdrawn from employment when their children were young, with the remainder leaving work on marriage or the birth of their first child. Only a small minority of the group had preschool-age children. The women were quite varied in the length of time they had been on home duties before doing the course/scheme (see Appendix 4.1 for further details). The women trainees had quite a low level of initial education, with just under half having primary education only. The group of rural women were varied in their labour market attachment; two were working part-time, two were on a course/scheme with the remainder on full-time home duties combined, in many cases, with part-time education courses. Most of those in home duties had withdrawn from the labour market on the birth of their first child. Three of the ten women had preschool-age children. Among the group working full-time in the home, all had preschool children, had left employment within the previous five years and had third-level education. The educational profile of the latter group is, therefore, more advantaged than the population of potential women returners as a whole (see Chapter 2).

Labour Force Withdrawal

Among the women working full-time at home, two had left paid employment on the birth of their first child while two had continued to work for a period after the birth of their first child. Their decision to leave paid employment was seen as representing a positive choice:

> I gave up work not because I had to but because I wanted to. I wanted to be with her [my daughter]. (Working full-time at home)

However, in the case of the two women who had continued to work, their decision also reflected the practical difficulties of combining paid work and childcare, especially in the absence of strong financial incentives to do so:

> I went back after the first was born for about two months and then realised that it really wasn't worth being back. Financially, it wasn't worth the cost of paying childcare, so I stopped. . . . The reduction of quality of life is not worth it, you are not taking any money home, and the quality of life would change because you spend the whole

> of your weekend running around cleaning, tidying, everything that when you were at home you would get done during the week, so your weekends are gone and for me this was a big thing. (Working full-time at home)

It was also felt that employers and work colleagues were not "family-friendly" in their attitude to women with children:

> Suddenly I was leaving at 5.00 and everybody else is turning around and staring and . . . my whole career plan was out of the window. I was not taken seriously once I had children. (Working full-time at home)

> That's what I found when I went back, that I was just treated as a completely different person to the person I'd been before I'd had the child. Immediately I wasn't in any line for any type of career progression. . . . You're looked at as a completely different person, and therefore you kind of think — is it worth putting all that effort in? Because I'm not going to get any further. . . . But then you begin to think, ah, it really isn't worth it because I'm not getting the same comeback from the job as I was before, so it's just not worth doing it. (Working full-time at home)

All of the women interviewed stated that they planned to return to work after their child(ren) started primary school:

> I will go back to work, but realistically speaking it will be when they're in a primary school. (Working full-time at home)

However, this was seen as somewhat uncertain:

> We could get there [to that point] and go, "I'm not going back to work now either". (Working full-time at home)

> I don't think I ever had a long-term plan on how long I planned to stay at home, 'cause I know it wasn't forever. I still don't know, I don't know what I'll do about going back to work. (Working full-time at home)

The return to work was also seen as contingent on being able to get a "suitable" job in terms of flexibility (see below).

Re-entering Education, Training and Employment

The profile of women who have returned to paid employment is considered in Chapter 5. However, the focus group interviews provided us with the opportunity to explore the motivations behind re-entering the labour market through education/training.[1] The reasons put forward by the women in our focus groups for getting involved in education/training can be broadly divided into "push" and "pull" categories. However, the reasons put forward by a lot of the women involved a combination of "push" and "pull" factors, as training was seen as meeting more than one of these purposes at the same time. Notwithstanding this, "push" factors were cited to a far greater extent as a reason for training compared with "pull" factors.

Where explanations involved "push" factors, the motivation to seek education/training stemmed mainly from a view that it offered an alternative to an unsatisfactory present situation. This contrasts with the explanations that involved "pull" factors, where the main motivation stemmed from an appreciation of the positive gains that training[2] could bring.

Push Factors

For some of the women, the "push" to train came from a desire to escape the isolation of home with a view to developing social contact with people outside of their immediate family. Even where women were already involved in part-time work at home (for example, childminding or taking in students), the desire to "get out of the house" and to increase social contact featured as an important reason for training:

---

[1] It should be noted that taking part in an education/training course did not necessarily lead to women remaining within the labour market (see below).

[2] Hereafter "training" is used to refer to both education and training courses while "trainee" is used to refer to all those who have taken part in education or training courses.

I had left my job six years earlier. I was at home minding my son and I took on students and all sorts just to make money and fill in time. I joined a lot of voluntary organisations just to keep in touch with people. Basically I wasn't a home person — I knew that even when I gave up work. So it was mainly because of lack of social contact with people. (Course participant)

I was working from home [doing] childminding. I'd done it for eleven years. So I decided I wanted a change, to get back out of the house, to work away from home. (Course participant)

I think every woman needs a few hours away from the children. They drive you mad all day . . .

[Other woman joins in]: Yeah, it's very lonely. You lose your confidence. (Course participant)

I was one of these women who stayed at home all my life and looked after my children and it was always there in the back of my mind that when these are done for then I'll go back to work. I thought, I don't really want to be at home all my life. I'd go crazy if I was to be in the house all the time. (Course participant)

Financial reasons relating to changed family circumstances were also important in the decision to seek training for some of the women. For the women in our focus groups, examples of such a change in circumstances included the onset of a disability, widowhood and marital separation. For these women, training was seen as an opportunity to improve on their present financial situation, which had declined dramatically since this change in circumstances occurred. The woman in the first excerpt was a widow and had worked as a cleaner until the onset of arthritis meant she could no longer continue with this type of employment. Her motivation to train was mainly financial, in the sense that she was paid for the course while being allowed to hold onto her widow's pension and secondary benefits:

> It was financial because I was widowed and I was only getting £70 or something like that a week. I was living alone and I had to run a whole house on that — everything, the mortgage, the whole lot. And the only help you could get I was told was help with the phone bill, twice a year. So to tell you the truth I was doing a bit of cleaning which I shouldn't have done, money into the hand. And that was handy. But when the course came up it was great because you got your benefits and you could still do the course. You got paid for the course — so it was financial with me. (Course participant)

Financial reasons, combined with the desire to be involved in something outside of homemaking, were cited by another woman in the focus group:

> I was 16 years at home and I'd had four babies in four years. And we had a very low income and we had a lot of money problems. The kids were getting to an age where they needed money and I was losing my sanity. I didn't go up to re-educate myself — it was to get out. And to be able to talk to my husband about something because all I seemed to talk about was what the kids said. (Course participant)

A change in financial circumstances due to marital separation emerged as another "push" factor. Financial reasons, combined with a desire to build confidence, were put forward by one of the women as the reason she sought training:

> I did not get any maintenance and I was getting my social welfare every week. I wasn't very well — I was heartbroken and I'd lost all my confidence. Anyway I was [attending a counselling service] . . . and after three or four years I was getting better. I was back in form and I was dying to get out to work. Of course it was because of the money, because I had to pay the mortgage and all that. But it was not just the money either. I wanted to get back with people who could support me and get back my confidence. (Course participant)

Pull Factors

One of the "pull" factors mentioned by one of the women in our study was the desire to learn new skills:

> Part of the reason I applied to the course is that everything now is keyboard skills. (Course participant)

An opportunity for a change of career was mentioned as a reason for training by another one of the women. Training was viewed as a two-fold opportunity: first, it offered the chance to change career, and second, the training structure was compatible with continuing family responsibilities:

> I was at home. I had actually stopped working for five years previously. I had worked all the time and then I stopped and I just decided that I wanted to get out of office work and do something different. Get a bit of money and just try it out and learn something new, basically. And I love cooking and I'm quite capable of doing it. I had worked for so long full-time and I decided to go back and train at something different, do something part-time so I would still be there for the kids when they came home at lunchtime. (Course participant)

There was also the recognition by another one of the women that training would provide an opportunity to find a better job:

> I know that I could probably earn a lot of money. Like these girls have been trained, I can't see why I can't be trained. (Course participant)

In sum, women's motivations to take part in education/training courses reflected a combination of their dissatisfaction with their present situation and a feeling that taking part in a course would improve their skills and employment prospects.

4.3 Perceived Barriers

A number of possible barriers hindering the return of women to education, training and/or employment were highlighted by both the service providers and women interviewed. These barriers centred on issues of information, access, self-confidence, childcare and other financial barriers, lack of flexibility in employment and course provision, and the absence of progression opportunities.

Information

For the women who returned to training, the search for information about training followed the actual decision to make the transition out of full-time homemaking. Their general feeling was that the availability of information was poor, with the onus on women themselves to go and find out what was suitable for their needs:

> I think you have to go out and look. Nobody's ever going to give it to you. You have to go out and look for it yourself. (Course participant)

Many of the women complained about the lack of information:

> There is not enough information given out to women. I recommended two friends to do it because they were asking, "How do you get on?" I told them and they went out and did it. But . . . they [other women] didn't know how to go about it. (Course participant)

Typically, the women relied on informal sources of information, for example asking friends/neighbours whom they knew to have knowledge of, or to have been involved in, training.

> I had all my friends demented asking them. I was just lucky. I had a friend who literally put me into her car and drove me up to the drop-in centre. (Course participant)

Similarly, another woman explained that she did not know where to find information about training and asked a neighbour who had already made the transition out of homemaking to work:

> I didn't know where to go. My neighbour returned to work and she told me to go to the Northside Partnership, which I did. (Course participant)

Sometimes women described that they found out about training opportunities quite accidentally:

> I'd been signing on for a year and I just got a letter from FÁS. I went down to FÁS and the girls said to me, "Is there any type of course you would like to do?" and I said, "What?" and she said, "We pay for any course you want to do". I was a year and I didn't know that. Nobody knows these things. It's not being fed in through the door. (Course participant)

Local newspapers also represented an important source of information:

> It was an advertisement I saw in the local newspaper, called the *Northside Post*. And that's when I rang up and they gave me an appointment and an interview. (Course participant)

> We were scanning papers all the time. And we saw this ad and said, "Oh God, that sounds good." So we decided to try that. And then we phoned up CERT. (Course participant)

From the accounts provided, it was clear that this type of information was not visible or readily accessible to a lot of women in their local areas and that there was great variability in the quality of the information available. As a result of their own experiences, the women trainees emphasised the importance of information being readily available to women at home. Suggestions for dissemination of information included advertisements in local newspapers, community centres, supermarkets and churches in addition to mail-shots through the door. It was also envisaged that public health nurses and GPs could play an important role in disseminating information to women.

While the women in full-time homemaking had not actively sought out information on returning to work, they were unclear about where to access such information and were not aware of the kinds of jobs and courses available in their local area. Given that all of these women had third-level education, it might be expected that access to information would pose more of a difficulty for the population of women returners as a whole. The women interviewed emphasised the need for a "one-stop" information source which would be locally based:

> Maybe it would be useful if there was somewhere that you could go even if you were vaguely thinking about going back to work, that you just wanted to have a chat and say, "Look this is what I've done, am I employable, how do I go about getting a job, what am I likely to earn, is there any childcare benefit?" (Working full-time at home)

Lack of information about local courses was also mentioned by the group of rural women. It was felt that information should be made available through:

> The local post office or local groups. Every area has good groups and they could be notified about what is available. Not six months after the course has been completed which is what happens out here. (Rural woman)

The need for information based on personal contact was recognised by one of the service providers:

> The thing about information, you can put a lot of information out there, paper information and whatever, and you can never be sure exactly how it's getting through. . . . An awful lot of people come into courses through word of mouth, through contact of friends, because somebody has said, I have done that and it's good. Or I know that

place and it's nice. So it really needs the personal touch. (VEC representative)

Another issue raised in the focus groups related to the lack of information on the consequences of training or employment participation for social welfare entitlements:

> You need . . . a degree in accountancy to figure out how to tell somebody what they would get, how the tax system affects them, what they would get to keep and then you bring childcare into the equation. . . . The mystery around retaining your medical card when you go back to work is unbelievable. (OPEN representative)

> There's not enough information on it . . . once women understand what their rights are in terms of social security and grants, for instance, where you can access all these and what your entitlements are, then you are one step further along. (Tesco representative)

The complexity of obtaining information on their entitlements was echoed in discussions with the women who had taken part in training courses.

In sum, lack of information was considered a significant barrier to women returning to education and/or employment by both the service providers and the women interviewed. Even those women who had successfully accessed education/training courses reported difficulties in finding out about the type of courses available and the consequences for their social welfare entitlements of taking part in such courses.

Access

The issue of access encompassed both geographical accessibility and criteria for entering particular education/training programmes. Firstly, regional variability in the provision of education/training courses was mentioned:

> There are some areas where there is fantastic work being
> done and there's other areas where you know they need
> the back-up and support to do something because
> there's nothing. (IFA representative)

Training and education service provision was perceived by the
women trainees in our study to be unevenly spread across all
women and all regions (principally disadvantaged versus other
areas within Dublin). Hearing about the experiences of women
who had been involved in community education, one woman
reported:

> We wouldn't even know how to go about that [setting up
> a course]. We haven't been involved in nothing like that.
> There is nothing like it [in our area]. (Course participant)

In addition, the availability of (certain types of) jobs was seen to
vary across regions:

> *Interviewer*: Would you think it's easy to get a job in [this
> area?]
>
> *Respondent*: Maybe full-time but not part-time. (Rural
> woman)
>
> We don't see much of the Celtic Tiger in the country ar-
> eas. (Rural woman)

Geographical location and inflexibility in the timing of courses
were also seen as making the return to work more difficult for
women in rural areas:

> There are not a lot of opportunities in the countryside. It's
> really financially not worthwhile driving into town for
> those couple of hours, the cost of the travel and the trav-
> elling time. You are talking about working from 10.00 to
> 1.30 to be back in time for the school. (Rural woman)

A second issue related to the priority given to those on the Live
Register in access to schemes:

> There are hundreds of thousands of women in this coun-
> try who . . . would love to get back to education and em-
> ployment and would love to do a FÁS course but because
> of the criteria around the Live Register, they are non-
> existent, these people, they can't access [training].
> (OPEN representative)

The importance of not distinguishing between different groups
on the basis of age, family status and work history in the right to
access courses was strongly voiced by the women:

> All women should definitely be entitled. It shouldn't be
> for certain people or groups. Some of the rules have
> changed but it seems over the years if you are a widow
> or if you are on disability the entitlements are different.
> Like it's mostly for lone parents — they get everything.
> (Course participant)

Women who experienced changes in their circumstances as a
result of widowhood or separation pointed to the inflexibility of
the system in responding to their needs. One woman, a widow,
explained that she had to wait a year before she was deemed
eligible to go into training:

> You have to be on the book as they say. You can't go into
> it straight away, which is wrong. (Course participant)

The role of gate-keepers was seen as crucial in facilitating access to courses:

> The very first person they meet is very important.
>
> *Interviewer*: Who would usually be their first point of con-
> tact?
>
> In a school, when they come in it could easily be the por-
> ter or it could be a teacher. . . . But whoever it is, the first
> port of contact needs to be encouraging and welcoming
> as well. You need to look at that, when people are com-
> ing in for their first session, that they are not put off and
> never come back again. (VEC representative)

One of the women trainees had a negative experience when she first approached her local training agency:

> I got there and went in and I was rattling. There was this man and he filled out loads of forms, blue forms. And he wrote down all that I was experienced in. I had no confidence because my marriage had just broken up and I had come back with two kids to my parents' house. I said to him, "There's all my qualifications — what do you think I should do?" And he said, "Well what do you want to do?" And I said that I didn't know what to do. I was trying to hold back the tears and he said, "There's a place on Baggot Street and you can go and get assessed" — you talk into some machine. I didn't go. That's not what I wanted to do. (Course participant)

Thirdly, the fact that entry to a course was often predicated on previous educational success was highlighted by some respondents:

> As regards the accessibility of courses to general people, that you don't have to have first-level qualifications, especially somebody who is more mature to have to go back and to have the question — as if you are a 17-year-old — "Have you got first-level qualifications?" and having to sit there and say, "No". (Tesco representative)

> I certainly feel that there are a lot of issues surrounding the openness and accessibility of third-level to women returners. (Private trainer)

The Mature Students' Officer in TCD stressed the way in which entry to third-level courses was now based on a broader set of skills rather than educational qualifications alone:

> We have just designed a new application form for Trinity . . . we have a section on activities other than educational. You could have [been the] chairperson of the parents' committee — that could involve a tremendous amount of skills, communication skills. . . . And they have space for

hobbies . . . they have to put in how that experience assists their development and growth.

However, the extent to which broader skills were sufficient to secure third-level entry appeared to vary by course:

> Each different department would have different requirements. . . . If you were going into sciences or a subject that requires Maths or has a special requirement, they will look for a certain level of education. (Mature Students' Officer, TCD)

The lack of recognition of women's "informal" skills was also seen as an issue influencing access to employment. Women, on the one hand, and employers, on the other, often failed to recognise the skills they had developed working in the home:

> I think the problem with a lot of women that stayed at home and had children [is] they don't understand that the skills they have in things like negotiating between teenage boys, or teenage family, or managing time . . . or just organisational skills actually can be transferred to a workplace environment. So actually they shouldn't lack confidence, they should actually revel in the experiences that they've had at home. And I think that's difficult to get across to women in general for whom it's just not perceived as being valuable work. (Tesco representative)

> I did some work for the Northside Partnership with women returners . . . and every single one of them had done something outside the home either in a paid or unpaid capacity. Whether it was the getting up at six o'clock in the morning to go and do the cleaning job in the local factory . . . or sitting on the children's school committee . . . and we don't value that either and they're huge skills. (Clondalkin Women's Network representative)

The women engaged in full-time home-making felt that they had acquired a range of skills as a result of their experience:

> I think I've learned a hell of a lot more being a mother than going to school. (Working full-time at home)

> I'm certainly a much more patient person than I ever was at work. (Working full-time at home)

> You do have a lot of patience, and you can do more things. You can be tired; when I used to complain that I was tired at work I wasn't really tired. I've never been as tired. But you can cope better at being tired and can still do things. (Working full-time at home)

However, they did not feel that any of the skills they had developed would be recognised in employment terms, unless they were to take a job in childcare:

> I don't think they'd [those skills] be appreciated. (Working full-time at home)

> But I think the only benefit we would have now if we were doing something in the childcare line; maybe giving talks or counselling or even working in a crèche or something, we'd be fine. But I don't think it's really helped us in an office or a corporate situation. (Working full-time at home)

In sum, lack of access to education, training and employment was seen to reflect geographical variability in the provision of education/training courses, differing criteria for accessing such courses along with the lack of recognition by employers of the skills and capacities developed by women working full-time in the home.

Self-confidence

The lack of self-confidence on the part of women was seen as a significant barrier in returning to the labour market:

> Confidence is by far the most important [factor], you know the confidence to feel, "God, you know, I could do it". (IFA representative)

> Women themselves, their own fear of maybe going back and failing again, not knowing what it's going to be like when they do go back prevents people. (VEC representative)

Women working full-time in the home described the loss of confidence that this entailed, and suggested that this became a greater barrier the longer one spent outside the labour market (see Chapter Five):

> My confidence is gone . . . I don't feel as confident since I stayed at home. (Working full-time at home)

> I think if you do want to go back, you've got to do it within a certain amount of time or then you do lose your confidence when you are so far out of it. (Working full-time at home)

Even where women had previous employment experience, the changing nature of the workplace meant that their skills were often (seen to be) obsolete:

> For older women there would certainly be an issue coming across in terms of confidence levels. . . . Particularly if they are coming into administrative roles, it's completely changed. They have to use the PC, Internet, e-mail, and it's completely different to the environment they left. And I think a lot of them are quite frightened by that and I don't think people realise that it is such a fundamental change for them. You know, their only skill might be to use the typewriter and now that's redundant. (Chambers of Commerce representative)

> There is a gap there from the point of view of people having the courage to come back in because the health service itself has changed a lot. (INO representative)

> Since I finished seven years ago there has been the Internet, and mobile phones. I worked for a solicitor for twelve years. That is gone now beyond recognition; peo-

ple don't write letters now, they just send e-mails. I don't
think I would like to go back to it; I don't want to be in an
office. . . . You wonder are you capable of doing the job,
are you as good as the person just out of school. (Rural
woman, working full-time at home)

Lack of self-confidence meant that women were reluctant to use
formal methods of job search and were more reliant on informal
sources of information:

The best thing that could happen is when somebody you
know who knows someone, to get a job that way, through
word of mouth rather than having to go out and look for a
job. . . . 'Cos it would be tough enough to go and do an
interview now — now, imagine what it would be like in
ten years' time. (Working full-time at home)

The incorporation of personal development components into
education/training provision was seen as crucial in boosting
women's confidence to re-engage with the workplace:

I definitely think that . . . we should have a core of this
personal effectiveness for the workplace and personal
matters, for you need to be more effective in your personal life and your relationships when you're negotiating
work. (Private trainer)

Childcare

The lack of childcare provision was seen as a major barrier to
women's participation in training and employment by all of
those interviewed:

I think the childcare issue is a major issue in terms of
people trying to go back and access training and education and then staying in the labour force, keeping your
job, and it's a huge, huge issue. (Chambers of Commerce representative)

If you're on a minimum wage job, you really can't afford to buy decent childcare and that's just the bottom line, that's the economic reality. (INOU representative)

Person 1: I suppose what is needed is something like the play-group but it's not long enough. Most jobs go on 'til after lunch if you are working part-time. Really you need something for the afternoon.

Person 2: Something affordable too.

Person 3: Childcare costs are so high, if you had a part-time job it's not worth your while working for money, except you want the social aspect. (Rural women's focus group)

The absence of formal provision meant that women were often reliant on family for childcare and these arrangements were liable to break down:

You see it all boils down to childcare. It does for me because I don't have anyone to mind them. Since my father died — he used to do a lot of babysitting for my sister and myself. But I don't have anybody there now. (Course participant)

I went back to work part-time in [company name] head office — I lasted seven weeks. My mum-in-law used to mind the kids but she got sick and she couldn't really mind them. So I went down to the social welfare and I said, "I have to stop, I have nobody to mind my kids." It was the time of the flu and she [my mother-in-law] just couldn't get the energy to mind three young children. (Course participant)

The need for childcare was seen as not only affecting women with younger children but as also having implications for women with school-going children. Responsibility for childcare also devolved to older women in their roles as grandmothers, which in turn inhibited their choices:

As more women are going out to work and as childcare is
in the situation that it is, that accessibility of it is so difficult, many younger women are falling back on their
mothers to look after the caring of their children and so
these older women are being inhibited from having access to part-time jobs, or full-time jobs, or whatever sort
of job, and they're not free to access the training. (Age
and Opportunity representative)

The provision of a childcare allowance for those on VTOS
courses was seen as a positive incentive for women returning to
education:

Certainly it means when you are offering a course you
can say that this [the allowance] is available. I think a lot
of women didn't come in even looking for courses before. They just took it for granted, well what am I going to
do, there is no help for childcare. Now they know there
is, so they are more likely to come in looking for a
course. . . . It won't remove all the barriers. But it certainly helps some women with childcare to get back in.
(VEC representative)

Even where childcare was provided, however, for example in
Rowlagh Women's Group, the extent of provision was often in-
adequate. As one of the women in Rowlagh explained:

We have crèche facilities in our group but there is only
eight places. On enrolment day, I mean, it's awful to have
to tell people that they have a place on the course but
they've no childcare.

The CERT representative reported that no childcare places
were provided at the Amiens Street Centre and that only four
childcare places were available in the Ballymun and Clondalkin
centres (see Chapter 3).

In sum, there was a degree of consensus that childcare
should be good quality, affordable and flexible in terms of the
hours provided. However, there was less agreement on the

most appropriate form of provision and how such provision should be funded. The women in full-time home-making stressed the need for good quality, flexible childcare. Their preferred mode of provision was either a childminder at home (although this option was seen as expensive) or workplace-based facilities:

> If some of the bigger companies had crèches at work . . . I think that would be so different if you could see your child during the day, you mightn't feel so bad about go-ing back to work. (Working full-time at home)

> It would be so much easier; if a child got sick, you could go so quickly to see them and back again. (Working full-time at home)

One of the service providers also felt that employers should be involved in the provision of childcare facilities:

> [Childcare] has to come from the employers as well as the training. There's no point in us providing training and childcare facilities and having nowhere to put them after it. It's unfair to the trainee, it's unfair to the children. . . . (CERT representative)

However, another felt that the primary responsibility rested with the state:

> Really the state needs to get far more involved in terms of subsidised supply. I mean we take it for granted the state plays a massive role in terms of primary education, for example. (INOU representative)

Financial Barriers

Financial barriers to returning to paid employment were mentioned in relation to childcare costs (see above). In addition, financial constraints were seen as influencing the choice between returning to education and moving directly into employment:

> It's very hard to come back into education and maybe
> spend ten hours a week on a course when you could be
> spending ten hours a week working and making some
> money for the home. And not only yourself, but explain-
> ing that to a partner as well, and children are looking for
> stuff. So the fact that a lot of women have been getting
> back into badly paid but part-time work in recent years
> because it's been there, has meant they are not attending
> classes. (VEC representative)

As a result, it was felt that payments should be available for
those attending education, as well as training, courses:

> Payment for people going back to courses is important.
> . . . If it's going to be a choice between that and getting
> a few hours' work, it's a very hard choice to make if you
> need the money. (VEC representative)

The payment of an allowance was seen as an important support
by the women who had taken part in training courses.

Flexibility

Existing education/training programmes were seen by some
respondents as inflexible in relation to hours and to content:

> In relation to the mainstream of training and education, a
> big issue . . . is the starting and finishing times of courses.
> I mean to expect someone to walk into a FÁS course at
> 8.30 in the morning when you're dropping your children
> to school. It's a particular issue for lone parents because
> there is no partner, but I mean it's the same for all par-
> ents. . . . I walk into some of the training centres and it's
> almost like walking into an assembly line or something
> and there is no recognition of individuality and [the fact
> that] we all learn differently. . . . There is no account
> taken of that and there is absolutely no account taken for
> special needs or literacy. (OPEN representative)

The difficulty of developing a flexible programme was stressed
by one of the service providers:

> I think it's a hard balance to get, it's trying to get a balance between something that is very flexible and moves, let's say, with the needs of the group themselves. And isn't too structured and laid down and gives people a chance to learn through the very fact that they are deciding what to learn themselves. . . . It has to be supportive and there has to be an element of guidance and direction while at the same time being very flexible. (VEC representative)

However, the FÁS representative countered that the Return to Work courses were more flexible than other schemes/courses, particularly as they were often based in the local community. Similarly, there had been some increase in the flexibility of CERT courses through the development of part-time and/or community-based provision:

> The timing has to be flexible because if they have children, they want to be able to leave them at school and pick them up, so you have to be able to facilitate at least one or the other. . . . The elementary one [courses], we can't be as flexible and that does cause a problem with childcare. (CERT representative)

Furthermore, a lack of flexibility in employer practices was seen as hindering the return of women to work, particularly in the context of the existing division of labour within the household:

> There is a list of people waiting for job-sharing . . . you get one hospital that will be really good, one employer will be really good, and you get another who almost uses it as a tool for control and they [the women] could be years waiting for it. (INO representative)

> It seems a lot of them [women returners] are maybe trading off flexible working hours against good pay. . . . 'Cause it's still the women who do the looking after the kids. (INOU representative)

An employer argued that this pattern sometimes reflected rigidity on the part of unions and/or existing workers in relation to flexible working hours and points of entry on pay scales:

> More and more they [women returners] are looking for part-time jobs but because of the inflexibility of our current workforce, because they are on full-time hours, it is very difficult to fit part-timers into the overall set-up because of the way you structure your business. . . . We're constrained by the fact that we can only have new starters coming in at one level. . . . They've got skills, customer service skills in particular, that we would value and would make us want to put them higher on the scale but the unions would be able to turn round and say, "no, that's not fair". (Tesco representative)

Women who were full-time in the home expressed the need for flexible working conditions if they were to return to work:

> A flexible kind of job maybe where . . . obviously they took into account that you would be off the odd day if the children were sick, that you might have to leave early some days or you might be coming in late a bit. A baby-friendly type of job. (Working full-time at home)

For the most part, this reflected a desire to return to work on a part-time basis, at least initially:

> I never want to go back to full-time employment, not with four children. You just want quality of life. Working full-time and overtime, I've done that now, and I don't want to go back to that. I want a job that I am not stressed out at. (Rural women's group)

> You want to break into work gently, not go straight to full-time. (Rural women's group)

> The hours would be a big factor in anything I decide to go into. I would pick stones if the hours were right. (Rural women's group)

However, the difficulty of caring for school-going children during the summer holidays was also mentioned:

> If I was going back to work, I wouldn't mind working full days, but I wouldn't go back, really, until the kids were at school. But . . . I'd like to be off when they're on holidays, so I would need a school-term job. (Working full-time at home)

The need for locally based employment was seen as more important for women with children:

> Commuting is a problem too. . . . I would like to go back to work but I wouldn't dream of going into the city again. It would have to be either local or going against the traffic. There's no way I would go into town. Then you see, what happens then is that the better paid jobs are in the city as well, so it's a Catch-22. (Working full-time at home)

A more flexible approach to parental leave and the development of family-friendly policies for male, as well as female, workers were also discussed:

> You should have a year [after the birth of your child], where your job is guaranteed, without a doubt, because three months or whatever it is, is not enough. (Working full-time at home)

> I mean there might be people who are ready after a year to go back, who aren't ready after three months. And then give up completely because they're not ready after three months. (Working full-time at home)

> Maybe men's working hours should change, they are all mostly from nine to six in the evenings. . . . It would be good if the men could work more around the women. (Rural woman)

It was acknowledged, however, that there was often a "trade-off" between more flexible working conditions and the pay/status of the job itself:

I think first of all when you are going part-time, well, you are not gonna go back into a senior position that you've been in before. (Working full-time at home)

I'd say that any job I wanted to do has to be full-time, I can't imagine getting away with doing what I want to do part-time. (Working full-time at home)

In sum, the women interviewed stressed the need for more flexible working conditions and course provision. In particular, they emphasised the importance of access to employment and training organised on a part-time and/or term-time basis.

Progression

Even when women had taken active steps to re-enter the labour market, it was felt that barriers to women remaining in the labour force may be evident. The need for support for those taking part in education/training was seen as crucial:

It's self-perception . . . the effect of which the small failure will bowl them over. . . . If you are thirty-odd and invested lots in it and every essay is very important . . . getting a poor mark really hits them badly, they seem to take it harder. (Mature Students' Officer, TCD)

Counselling support was considered necessary for course participants with particular problems or difficulties. In addition, progression from a course to further training or employment was seen as dependent on the availability of appropriate guidance and follow-up support. Lack of progression was also seen as relating to lack of self-confidence on the part of the trainee:

It's always been an issue that a lot of people kind of go around in circles, or get cosy somewhere and don't really want to move on. Or that centres themselves kind of feel rather than moving someone on to another centre that offers another course they'll put on the course themselves. (VEC representative)

Many service providers highlighted the disjuncture between expectations and reality as a factor in women's leaving the labour force after initially re-entering employment:

> I think in nursing the expectation would be that if you're out of it ten or fifteen years that things would have improved in terms of how you're treated. . . . Nothing has changed. The attitudes are still the same and that's the problem. (INO representative)

> One bad experience of work is the end of it . . . it can spell the end of progress. Expectations can be very high as well leaving a course because you're training them to best practice and then they go out to industry and maybe it's not best practice and, end of story: "I'm not working here". (CERT representative)

> Expectations that people have about work, it is critical that they are taken into account in terms of not just perceived barriers to work but actual treatment when they're there. (Forfás representative)

Some of the difficulty was seen to reflect less flexibility in the wider workforce than in course/scheme provision:

> There are reasons why lone parents and other parents, but in particular lone parents, are attracted to Community Employment — the part-time, the local, the childcare, and that isn't reflected in the world of work. So actually, nationally, lone parents do not have a good progression from CE into full-time employment because the workforce doesn't accommodate part-time, local, childcare. (OPEN representative)

> The results of our providing crèche spaces in other centres shows that people don't necessarily go to work after having their crèche space. They'll have their crèche space while they train but then they can't go to work anyway because they've no crèche space. (CERT representative)

The gendered division of labour within the household was also highlighted as a potential barrier for women attempting to move from a course into employment:

> The older ones, it can be husbands' attitudes, where they don't mind them going out to do a course but going to work is a different matter when my dinner should be on the table and has been for the last twenty years or thirty years. (CERT representative)

> A lot of women voice that to me, they say, "If I am going to be the income-earner here, the marriage could go." (Private trainer)

> Sometimes it can be difficult, maybe at home if there is a partner who doesn't see the importance of this for the woman and who doesn't appreciate it. (VEC representative)

These views were echoed by the FÁS representative who mentioned that lack of support from partners was a barrier to progression for some women.

The lack of career progression for women returners was also emphasised; this was attributed both to employers' failure to provide continuing training and to women's reluctance to "push" for promotion and training opportunities:

> Employers have begun to create part-time places. . . . And when they do get them in, I think there may be an issue with career progression, especially for older women. I think most employers do provide initial training . . . but I'm not sure what space there is, if someone comes in and they're 45 or 50, how much progression do they make? . . . [But] I think it is more . . . the women [need] to come up to them and say, "I think I would like to do X, could I ever go on that training course?", but it's getting the women to take to that point of actually going up and asking. (Chambers of Commerce representative)

> They may get the training initially but then they are ex-
> pected to function like everyone else. . . . It's lack of sup-
> port once they're back in. (INO representative)

It appears, therefore, that the successful reintegration of women into the labour force depends not only on ease of initial access but on longer-term support and training in order to facilitate their career progression.

Actual Progression Patterns among Women Trainees

The women in our focus groups had taken a number of different routes since their involvement in training or education. Of the 15 "trainees", seven were in paid employment,[3] two were on a scheme, two were combining full-time home-making with on-going participation in part-time courses and four were in full-time home duties.

One of the main findings to emerge from the research was that for many women, the particular training or education "episode" represented just one point along what might be seen as a continuum of learning. In other words, many of the women had previously participated in a number of courses/programmes and were continuing with training up to the present. Furthermore, this training was spread across a variety of agencies (including CERT and FÁS) and types of courses/programmes. All in all, most of the women in our study imparted a keen interest in further education and training; this was seen as an opportunity for self-development, to set an example for, and to be able to participate in, their own children's education and to improve their employment opportunities. However, for many of the women in our study, constraints associated with hours, child-care and access meant that the option of the training/course of their choice had to be postponed.

Seven of the women had moved into paid work since their involvement in training. An important factor in helping the

---

[3] The type of work entered by returners is discussed in Chapter 6 below, using a national sample.

women to make this transition was the confidence-building and job preparation help they received as part of the training:

> We had a day, Thursday, and we used to go through all the jobs, and we could use the phone, the fax and we could apply for a job. I rang one day, I wasn't going to ring, but I rang and they said to come for an interview and I got the job. (Course participant)

> They wrote out CVs and everything and we did mock interviews. I wasn't selling myself at the interview and she [the trainer] did a special interview with me. (Course participant)

The general view amongst the women who had moved into employment was that they would not have been able to do their particular jobs without the training. This was expressed by one of the older women in the group who had never used computers before the training and was now in a job that involved inputting data onto a computer:

> I never would have known anything about computers before I started the course. I rang up and thanked [the trainer]. Before when I opened the paper and saw ECDL I would have said, "I wonder what's that?" I never thought I would understand it. (Course participant)

Of the 15 women, just two had moved into full-time employment; one of these women actually wanted a part-time job:

> I was very adamant that I wanted a part-time job but I'd no success because there's so many people applying for it. So I'm working flexi-time but I try to do from 8.00 to 4.00. (Course participant)

The women who moved into employment had a slightly higher educational level than those who were in further training or on home duties; half of those in home duties and both of those on schemes had primary education only compared with one out of seven of the employed women. Interestingly, those in employment did not differ markedly from the other groups in terms of their childcare responsibilities. However, it is worth noting that women with pre-school children formed a small minority of focus group participants taking part in education/training in the first place.

4.4 Conclusions

A number of common issues were raised by service providers, women who had taken part in education/training, and women working full-time in the home. It was felt that there was a lack of information about the courses and schemes available and that dissemination of information should take place locally, preferably using informal channels. Access to education/training was seen to be variable across areas and across different groups of women. It was felt that provision should be more flexible in this respect. Lack of suitable childcare was seen as perhaps the biggest potential barrier to women's re-entry to the workforce. There was a consensus that childcare should be good quality, affordable and flexible. However, there were differences between respondents regarding the appropriate mode of provision and funding. Lack of self-confidence was also perceived as an important barrier and the inclusion of self-development components in training/education was seen as crucial in boosting women's confidence to re-enter employment. Those interviewed emphasised the need for flexibility on the part of course providers and employers in relation to women returners. In addition, the need for ongoing support for women who have returned to education, training and/or employment was stressed.

This chapter has focused on the perceived barriers to women's (successful) re-entry to the labour force. Some of the women trainees had, however, overcome these barriers to move from a course or scheme into paid employment. The factors associated with successful re-integration into the labour market are explored further in the next chapter.

Appendix 4.1: Profile of Focus Group Participants

Table 4.1: Age-group of Participants

	Education/ Training Course Participants	Rural Women	Women on Home Duties
25–35	4	2	3
36–45	5	5	1
46–55	4	2	0
Over 55	2	1	0
Total	15	10	4

Table 4.2: Highest Level of Formal Education

	Education/ Training Course Participants	Rural Women	Women on Home Duties
Primary	6	0	0
Lower sec.	5	4	0
Upper sec.	4	6	0
Third-level	0	0	4
Total	15	10	4

Table 4.3: Length of Time on Home Duties

	Education/ Training Course Participants[1]	Rural Women[2]	Women on Home Duties
≤ 5 years	5	1	4
6–10 years	4	1	0
11–15 years	2	1	0
15+ years	4	3	0
Total	15	6	4

[1] Time on home duties before entering education/training course.

[2] For those women in full-time home duties.

Chapter 5

THE FACTORS ASSOCIATED WITH WOMEN RETURNING TO THE WORKFORCE, EDUCATION AND TRAINING

5.1 Introduction

In analysing the factors associated with labour market participation among returners, it is useful to recognise that the transition to work is a function of two decision-making processes conducted, on the one hand, by those supplying their labour, and on the other, by those seeking to hire labour. The demand side of the labour market is primarily driven by the size and nature of demand in the economy and we have noted already that the period since 1993 has seen a dramatic increase in labour demand. The most dynamic sectors of the labour market during that period have been in the services sector, with the result that employment growth has been fastest in those sectors, a factor which may be related to the substantial increase in women in employment in the past decade or so in Ireland (O'Connell, 2000). The sheer scale of employment demand is not, however, the only factor which influences labour market entry and participation. The organisation of work, including the provision of part-time and other forms of atypical or flexible working arrangements, may also influence the numbers participating in the labour force. This is a particularly important issue for women, who are more likely to seek to combine paid work in the labour market with domestic and caring work in the home.

On the supply side of the labour market, studies of female labour market participation have suggested a host of factors which may influence entry, including personal characteristics, such as age and educational attainment, household factors, including partners and children, as well as labour-market-related variables, including previous work experience and the incentive structure shaped by the social welfare system. However, studies of female participation in Ireland are generally based on cross-sectional analyses of who is in or out of the labour market at a particular point in time. While they assume transition processes in and out of the labour market, they do not model either transition directly. In this chapter, we directly assess the factors that influence transitions from home duties into work/education/ training/employment schemes. We focus mainly on the supply side, looking at individual and household factors but include year and geographical location as measures of demand.

5.2 Descriptive Analysis of Transitions over Time

For those in home duties at each survey (*t*) we identify four different destination states in the following year (*t+1*); these are: at work; in education/training; non-employed seeking work; non-employed not seeking work. The non-employed category includes those women who in *t+1* define themselves as in home duties, unemployed or retired.

The year-on-year transition matrices for women in home duties into these four destinations are reported in Tables 5.1 to 5.3. The proportion of women in home duties moving into work each year remained relatively stable at about 7 per cent from 1994 to 1997, but increased to almost 12 per cent in 1998–1999, an increase which probably reflects the effects of labour shortages at the end of the 1990s. Throughout the period, those seeking at time *t* have a much higher rate of employment at time *t+1* than women who were not actively looking for work.

The proportion moving into what might be intermediate positions, i.e. training, education or government employment schemes, has hovered around two per cent for the whole time period. It is interesting to note that a significant proportion of those in home duties who are searching in year 1 have suspended this search by year 2; for example, half of the women seeking work in wave 1 had stopped searching in wave 2. In other years, the percentage quitting job search dropped to between 30 and 40 per cent. This may be a response to a lack of success in finding work or may reflect a change in orientation to the labour market.

Table 5.1: Transition Matrix for Women in Home Duties, 1994–95 and 1995–96 (%)

Status in (*t+1*)	In Home Duties 1994 (*t*)			In Home Duties 1995 (*t*)		
	Seeking	*Not seeking*	*All*	*Seeking*	*Not seeking*	*All*
Employed/ Self-emp	18.0	5.4	6.5	13.5	6.1	6.7
Training/Emp Scheme/Ed.	7.5	1.8	2.3	15.6	2.4	3.5
Non-employed, seeking	22.6	3.1	4.8	31.3	2.4	4.6
Non-employed, not seeking	51.9	89.8	86.4	39.6	89.1	85.2
	100.0	100.0	100.0	100.0	100.0	100.0
Unweighted N	*114*	*1,395*	*1,509*	*73*	*1,182*	*1,255*
Chi-square	*P < .001*					

Table 5.2: Transition Matrix for Women in Home Duties, 1996–97 and 1997–98 (%)

Status in (t+1)	In Home Duties 1996 (t)			In Home Duties 1997 (t)		
	Seeking	Not seeking	All	Seeking	Not seeking	All
Employed/ Self-emp	23.6	5.9	6.7	23.4	5.6	7.0
Training/Emp Scheme/Ed.	3.6	1.9	1.9	3.9	2.4	2.5
Non-employed, seeking	40.0	6.1	7.8	36.4	2.5	5.2
Non-employed, not seeking	32.7	86.2	83.6	36.4	89.5	85.3
	100.0	100.0	100.0	100.0	100.0	100.0
Unweighted N	54	1,074	1,128	58	880	938
Chi-square	P<.001			P<.001		

Table 5.3: Transition Matrix for Women in Home Duties, 1998–99 (%)

Status in 1999 (t+1)	In Home Duties 1998 (t)		
	Seeking	Not Seeking	All
Employed/Self-emp.	19.4	11.4	11.8
Training/Emp. scheme/Ed.	11.1	2.1	2.6
Non-employed, seeking	25.0	1.6	2.7
Non-employed, not seeking	44.4	84.9	82.9
	100.0	100.0	100.0
Unweighted N	35	736	771
Chi-square	P < .001		

Long-term Transition Rates

Tables 5.1 to 5.3 show the annual transition rates between home duties and employment. However, because we have panel data for six years, it is also possible to examine transition rates over a longer time period. In Table 5.4, we outline the proportion of women in home duties in 1994 who make the transition to work at any point up to 1999 (with the caveat that we do not observe cases in which a job is entered and left again in between annual surveys). When we look at transitions over the longer period, we see that over one-fifth (21 per cent) of those in home duties in 1994 made a transition into unsupported employment at some time over the six-year observation period. We also present the transition rates for the subset of the women who responded to all six surveys: 27 per cent of this group are found to have made a transition from home to employment by 1999. These results em-phasise the fluidity of women's employment status described in Chapter 2 of this report; over a quarter of women in home duties at the start of the survey period had experienced at least one spell of employment over a six-year period.

Table 5.4: Percentage of Women in Home Duties in 1994 who made Transition to Employment between 1994 and 1999

	Present in Any Two Surveys	In All Six Surveys[1]
No transition to work	76.5	72.9
Yes, transition from home to work	23.5	27.1
	100.0	100.0
Base N	*1,743*	*950*

[1] Weighted by six-wave longitudinal weight.

5.3 Profile of Returners

In this section we provide a profile of the women who moved from home duties into work between any two of the six survey years. For this initial analysis we do not consider transitions into education, training or supported employment. We compare the characteristics of those who make the transition into work to women who remained non-employed and we confine the sam-ple to women in home duties in 1994 who responded in all six waves of the survey. The results refer to the women's character-istics in the first year of the observation period, i.e. 1994. Of course, some of these characteristics, such as age of youngest child or time out of the labour market, change over time and the cross-sectional tables cannot deal with this complexity. Therefore in section 5.4 below we construct transition models which take into account changes in women's characteristics over time.

Labour Market and Educational Profile of Returners

The vast majority (89 per cent) of women returners have previous work experience; this is identical to the proportion for women who did not exit home duties (Table 5.5). It is also of interest that the proportion who made the transition into work over the six years is the same for those with and without experience. Among those who have had a job, there is a significant gap in the length of time out of employment between returners and non-returners (Table 5.6). Twelve per cent of women in home duties who returned to work had been out of employment for less than two years when interviewed in 1994, compared to only five per cent of non-returners.[1] This is not to say that those who have spent a very long period in the home have no chance of returning to employment. Even among those who had been out of the labour market more than 20 years in 1994, 16 per cent made a transition to work at some point over the six years observed.

---

[1] It should be noted that if we include women who enter and leave the surveys, and who were not in home duties in 1994, the incidence of recent work experience among returners is higher. One explanation is that the current selection excludes women who entered home duties following the 1994 interview, who would have very recent work experience. These groups are included in the models below.

Table 5.5: Previous Work Experience among Returners and Non-returners, Measured in 1994 (%)

	Returners	Non-returners	Transition Rate for Group
Work experience	89.0	89.4	27.0
No experience	11.0	10.6	27.9
All	100.0	100.0	27.1
Unweighted N	*246*	*703*	

Notes: Tables 5.5 to 5.11 are weighted to take account of sample attrition. "Returners" made transition from home duties to work at any time between 1994 and 1999. "Non-returners" did not make transition from home duties to work during observation period. Only includes women who completed all six annual surveys.

Table 5.6: Time Since last Job, Measured in 1994 (%)

	Returners	Non-returners	Transition Rate for Group
Less than 2 years	11.6	5.3	45.1
2–4.9 years	17.6	11.4	36.9
5–9.9 years	16.3	14.3	30.2
10–14.9 years	17.8	14.4	31.9
15–20 years	16.5	13.9	30.9
Over 20 years	20.2	40.7	15.8
All	100.0	100.0	27.4
Unweighted N	*226*	*607*	

See notes to Table 5.5.

The educational level of returners is relatively low: 38 per cent have no qualifications, a further 28 per cent have Intermediate Certificate level qualifications and 34 per cent have achieved Leaving Certificate level or higher (Table 5.7). This lack of formal qualifications is likely to influence the type of jobs that the women move into. The quality of employment entered is investigated in the next chapter.

Although the educational qualifications of many returners are low, they compare favourably with the levels reported by those in home duties who did not return to work. Among the women who remained non-employed, 46 per cent had no qualifications. Examining the transition rates for the different educational groups, it is clear that the probability of making a transition into work is much higher among women with third-level education, where almost 40 per cent of the group will have returned to work over the six years. This compares to a transition rate of only 22 per cent among women in home duties with no qualifications.

Table 5.7: Educational Qualifications of Returners and Non-returners, Measured in 1994 (%)

	Returners	Non-returners	Transition Rate for Group
No Quals	37.9	49.6	22.2
Inter Level	28.1	21.2	33.2
Leaving Level	27.8	25.7	28.8
Tertiary	6.2	3.5	39.5
	100.0	100.0	27.2
Unweighted N	*246*	*697*	

See notes to Table 5.5

Before moving on to family and demographic factors, we briefly examine the welfare profile of respondents. This issue is seen as being important as it is sometimes argued that the receipt of a state benefit will act as a disincentive to employment; it is also important in highlighting the extent to which returners have access to employment supports that are rationed by welfare status. The results show that the great majority of returners (79 per cent) were not receiving any state benefits when interviewed in 1994. The largest group of benefit claimants were those receiving lone parent's benefits, who made up 11 per cent of returners. These were followed by those on unemployment benefit/assistance who made up a further 6 per cent. The transi-

tion rates of those claiming unemployment benefits were significantly higher than any other group (40 per cent returned to work
over the study period). Unemployment benefit claimants may
have other characteristics that make them more likely to return,[2]
or perhaps receive extra assistance to get back to work. Those
on lone parent's benefits have a transition rate close to the average, while those on pensions and sickness/disability benefits
have a low transition rate.

**Table 5.8: Receipt of Benefit in 1994 among Returners and
Non-returners (%)**

	Returners	**Non-returners**	**Transition Rate for Group**
No benefits	78.8	71.2	29.1
Unemp. benefits	6.1	3.3	40.4
Lone Parent's benefit	11.3	9.5	23.8
Sick/Disability benefits	0.8	3.6	7.8
Pension/Survivor's benefits	1.6	6.8	7.7
Other	3.2	3.7	24.1
	100.0	100.0	27.1
Unweighted N	*246*	*704*	

See notes to Table 5.5

Demographic and Family Characteristics of Returners

Women who made a transition from home duties into work are
found to be significantly younger than women who remained
non-employed: 34 per cent of returners were aged under 35
years in 1994 compared to 24 per cent of the non-returners
(Table 5.9). Furthermore, 29 per cent of the non-returners were
aged 55–64 years in 1994 and were therefore approaching retirement age. It is not surprising, therefore, that the transition

---

[2] For example, receipt of these benefits requires recent employment experience.

rate for women in the 55 to 64 age group is very low, with only 5
per cent making a transition to work over the six years.

*Table 5.9: Age Profile of Returners and Non-returners,
Measured in 1994 (%)*

	Returners	Non-returners	Transition Rate for Group
Under 25	8.0	5.5	34.8
25 to 34yrs	25.9	18.6	34.1
35 to 44yrs	38.5	22.3	39.0
45 to 54yrs	23.8	24.6	26.4
55 to 64yrs	3.9	29.0	4.8
	100.0	100.0	27.1
Unweighted N	*246*	*704*	

See notes to Table 5.5

The younger age profile of returners is likely to influence the
family characteristics that we observe. Returners are more
likely than non-returners to have pre-school children and those
with young children are somewhat more likely to return to
work. This finding is somewhat counter-intuitive, given the evidence of childcare barriers emphasised by the focus group
participants. In the models below we will examine whether this
effect remains when we control for age and time since last job.
The models also look at additional family characteristics such as
partner's employment status and elder care.

Table 5.10: Children under Five Years in 1994 (%)

	Returners	Non-returners	Transition Rate for Group
No	69.2	78.4	25.0
Yes	30.8	21.6	32.2
	100.0	100.0	27.1
Unweighted N	*246*	*704*	

See notes to Table 5.5

The final demographic characteristic we examine is geographical location. We have divided the information on household location into three categories. The rural group consists of those in villages with a population of less than 1,500 and in open country. The small and medium town category consists of towns of 1,500 or more. "City" includes those located in Waterford, Galway, Limerick, Cork and Dublin cities, and those in Dublin county.

Returners are more likely to be living in a city compared to non-returners (Table 5.11). The transition rates for women in cities is also somewhat higher than in those in non-urban locations, which is likely to reflect the greater job opportunities available to city dwellers. These results reinforce the views of women in the rural focus group reported in Chapter 4.

Table 5.11: Regional Distribution of Returners and Non-returners, Measured in 1994 (%)

	Returners	Non-returners	Transition Rate for Group
Rural (<1500)	36.6	42.0	24.4
Small/Med Town	20.0	23.2	24.2
City	43.4	34.9	31.6
	100.0	100.0	27.1
Unweighted N	*246*	*704*	

See notes to Table 5.5

The models will test the independent impact of these factors on transitions controlling for other characteristics. These tables have focused on characteristics at the start of the study period in 1994, but the models are designed to take account of changes in these factors over time; they will also provide additional information on the transition from home duties to education/training and employment schemes.

5.4. A Multivariate Approach to Transitions to Work

Table 5.12 shows a logistic model of transitions from home duties to work between successive waves of the panel survey from 1994–1999. The approach is to model the conditional probability of moving out of home duties given that exit has not already occurred and depending on the values of selected covariates.

Table 5.12: Logistic Regression of Transition from Home Duties to Work

	Coefficient	Std. Error
Intercept	−1.551***	0.403
Seeking Work	0.896***	0.154
Age < 25	*Ref.*	
Age 25–34	−0.180	0.291
Age 34–44	−0.405	0.315
Age 45–54	−0.939**	0.352
Age 55+	−1.767***	0.386
No Qualification	*Ref.*	
Junior Certificate	0.221	0.136
Leaving Certificate	0.191	0.141
Tertiary Education	0.754***	0.210
1994	*Ref.*	
1995	−0.060	0.156
1996	0.407**	0.151
1997	0.018	0.168
1998	0.399*	0.164
Married/with partner	*Ref.*	
Separated, Divorced or Widowed	0.172	0.354
Never Married	−0.279	0.392
No children aged under 12 years	*Ref.*	
Youngest child under 5 years	−0.630***	0.185
Youngest child aged 5–12 years	−0.141	0.153

Table 5.12 continued

	Coefficient	Std. Error
Partner working	−0.004	0.134
Caring for relative or other	−0.166	0.174
< 2 years out of labour market	*Ref.*	
2–5 years out of labour market	−0.816***	0.178
5–10 years out of labour market	−1.276***	0.191
10–15 years out of labour market	−1.393***	0.209
15–20 years out of labour market	−0.758***	0.253
>20 years out of labour market	−1.219***	0.206
Ever worked	0.352	0.196
Years working	0.839*	0.339
Education or training last year	0.104	0.227
No social welfare benefits	*Ref.*	
Pension	−0.036	0.456
Unemployment	−0.067	0.229
Sickness/Disability	−1.437**	0.465
Lone Parent	−0.082	0.368
Family Income Supplement	−0.453	0.496
Social Welfare Scheme	−0.332	0.324
City Resident	0.359***	0.107
N of cases	*5,833*	
−2 Log likelihood (intercept only)	*3,207.99*	
−2 Log likelihood (final)	*2,859.34*	
Nagelkerke R²	*0.140*	
* p < .05; ** p < .01; *** p < .001		

Discrete time models divide respondents' work histories into independent observations for each unit of time (in this analysis each year). In each year we record the response variable (employment status) and the values of time-constant variables such as sex and time-varying covariates such as age of youngest child. The duration of spell until exit is noted in the variable TIMEOUT. For those with previous work experience, this meas-

ures the time between the interview date at time 1 (*t*) and the
date when the last job finished (this is calculated each year).
For those with no previous work experience TIMEOUT is equal
to the total years spent in home duties measured at *t*. In the
models, TIMEOUT is divided into six categories, with less than
two years out as the reference category. As in the multivariate
analysis of job seeking in Chapter 2, the data consist of cross-
sectional information for each individual pooled over each of
the six interviews from 1994 to 1999.

In discrete time models, the unit of analysis becomes the
year rather than the individual. In our sample, 1,850 women
were in home duties in at least one of the surveys, and were observed in at least two consecutive waves of the survey between
1994 and 1999.[3] This produced 6,117 person-years to analyse. If
an individual experienced more than one transition, all transitions were included in the model.

Having been seeking work at the previous interview has a
positive and significant effect on the probability of accomplishing a transition to work. Older women — those aged over 45 —
were less likely to move from home duties to work. Education is
important. Women who have attended third-level education
were more likely to move from home duties to work, but those
at lower education attainment levels did not differ from the reference category, those with no qualifications. Timing is also
important, and women were more likely to make a transition to
work in 1996 and 1998 than they were in 1994, perhaps reflect-
ing the improvement in labour market demand in those years.
The other measure of demand — geographical location — also
proved significant. Women resident in urban areas (Waterford
or larger) are more likely to accomplish a transition to work.

With regard to household characteristics, marital status has
no impact on the probability of moving into employment. Nei-

---

[3] We re-ran the models restricting the sample to those who were present in all
six waves. The results were broadly similar; however, we decided to maxi-
mise the number of transitions included in the model.

ther does the presence of a working spouse. We also investigated the influence of the presence of a non-working spouse, but found no statistically significant effect (results not reported in Table 5.12). The presence of young children does influence the transition to work. Women with youngest children aged less than 5 years are less likely to make the transition from home duties to work than those with no children under 12. However, having children aged 5–12 does not affect the transition probability, when all other variables are taken into account. Caring for elderly or other relatives in the household has no effect on the transition probability.

Years out of the labour market, our time variable, had a negative impact on the probability of a transition to work. The size of the effect fell among those who had been out of the labour market for 15-20 years. This pattern may be related to child-bearing and rearing, suggesting that the negative effect of time out of the labour market may be offset by some women returning to work after completing child-rearing. Years working, expressed as a proportion of total time elapsed since age ten, had a positive impact on the probability of entering employment. However, participation in education or training in the past year has no effect — a variable which we did find to positively influence job-seeking. Receipt of social welfare payments in respect of sickness or disability has a negative impact on the transition to work, which may be due to additional barriers to employment for this group or an inability to take up paid work. This is the only type of welfare payment which influenced the transition.

Work versus Education or Training

The options open to women engaged in home duties are not confined to a choice between work and home. As we can see from the transition matrices reported above, they can also participate in education and training, an option which may be an initial step in the return to the labour force in some cases. Given the possibility that education or training can serve as an intermediate stage in the move from home duties into the labour force, it is useful to develop a statistical model of the alternative destinations understood in terms of competing risks or outcomes.

Table 5.13 presents the results of a multinomial logistic analysis of the probability of moving from home duties in any given year to either (1) work, or (2) education, training or state-sponsored temporary employment scheme, versus remaining in home duties, in any subsequent year, from 1994 to 1999.

Table 5.13: Multinomial Logistic Regression of Transition to Work or Education/Training/Employment Scheme versus Remaining in Home Duties

	At Work		Educ/Training/ Emp. Scheme	
	Coeffi- cient	*Std. Error*	*Coeffi- cient*	*Std. Error*
Intercept	−1.499***	0.405	−3.689***	0.739
Seeking work	0.952***	0.155	0.909**	0.283
Partner working	−0.014	0.135	−0.466	0.302
Caring for relative or other	−0.185	0.174	−0.604	0.435
Educ/Training in last 12 mths	0.183	0.228	1.079**	0.343
Years working	0.862*	0.340	0.732	0.715
City	0.361**	0.108	0.155	0.226
Ever worked	0.346	0.196	0.036	0.372
Age < 25	*Ref.*			
Age 25–34	−0.211	0.293	−0.459	0.456
Age 35–44	−0.404	0.316	0.309	0.527
Age 45–54	−0.943**	0.353	0.195	0.636
Age 55+	−1.789***	0.387	−1.413	0.825
No Qualification	*Ref.*			
Junior Certificate	0.235	0.136	0.597*	0.289
Leaving Certificate	0.213	0.142	0.725*	0.295
Tertiary	0.770***	0.211	0.618	0.547

Table 5.13 continued

	At Work		Educ/Training/ Emp. Scheme	
	Coeffi- cient	*Std. Error*	*Coeffi- cient*	*Std. Error*
1994	*Ref.*			
1995	−0.054	0.156	0.072	0.305
1996	0.417	0.151	0.228	0.315
1997	0.019	0.169	−0.094	0.344
1998	0.392	0.165	−0.338	0.398
Married/with partner	*Ref.*			
Separated/Divorced/Widowed	0.127	0.355	−0.891	0.702
Never married	−0.254	0.393	−0.044	0.656
No children under 12 yrs of age	*Ref.*			
Youngest child under 5	−0.650***	0.185	−0.650	0.376
Youngest child 5–12yrs	−0.150	0.154	−0.323	0.326
< 2 yrs out of labour market	*Ref.*			
2–5 yrs out of labour market	−0.844***	0.179	−0.487	0.339
5–10 yrs out of labour market	−1.308***	0.192	−0.654	0.355
10–15 yrs out of labour market	−1.429***	0.209	−0.861*	0.412
15–20 yrs out of labour market	−0.798***	0.196	−0.854*	0.438
>20 yrs out of labour market	−1.265***	0.206	−1.786**	0.492
No social welfare benefits	*Ref.*			
Pension/ Survivor	0.062	0.457	−17.420	7189.6
Unemployment	0.068	0.231	1.773***	0.344
Sickness/ Disability	−1.438	0.465	0.046	0.618
Lone Parent	0.016	0.368	1.875**	0.647
Family Income Supplement	−0.470	0.497	−18.680	0.000
Social Welfare scheme	−0.329	0.325	−0.772	1.032
N of cases	*5,883*			
−2 log likelihood (intercept only)	*4,140.76*			
−2 log likelihood (final)	*3,581.15*			
Nagelkerke R²	*0.179*			
* p < .05; ** p < .01; *** p < .001				

With regard to the probability of moving from home duties to work versus remaining in home duties, the analysis effectively replicates the results reported in Table 5.12. Women who were seeking work in any year are more likely to be in employment in the following year. Women aged over 45 engaged in home duties are less likely to make the transition to work, but those in other age groups do not differ significantly from those aged under 25. Women in home duties who have attended third-level education are more likely to move to employment than those with lower levels of education. Marital status does not influence the probability of moving to employment, and neither does caring for an elderly or other relative.

As in the simpler model, years out of the labour market had a negative impact on the probability of a transition to work, and the size of the effect fell among those who had been out of the labour market for 15–20 years. Years working, expressed as a proportion of total time elapsed since age ten, also has a positive impact on the probability of entering employment. Receipt of sickness- or disability-related social welfare payments has a negative effect on the probability of moving into employment, and urban location has a positive effect.

The results for the contrast between being engaged in education, training, or a state-sponsored temporary employment scheme versus remaining in home duties in the subsequent year are presented in the final three columns of Table 5.13. Women who were seeking work in year 1 were more likely to be in education, training or an employment scheme than in home duties in year 2. Older women, aged over 55, were less likely to enter education or training. Marital status did not influence transition to education or training. Neither did the presence of young children, nor caring for an elderly or other relative.

Those with Junior or Leaving Certificate levels of education were more likely to enter an education, training or temporary employment scheme than those with no qualifications. However, those with higher levels of education were not. This may suggest some gaps in the provision of such programmes for women in home duties at both extremes of the educational distribution.

Women who had been out of the labour market for 10 years or more were less likely to enter education, training or a temporary employment scheme than those who had left the labour market more recently. Participation in education or training in the previous year had a positive effect on the transition to education or training, although this effect should be interpreted with caution, since in some cases the participation in education in the previous year may have continued through the subsequent year, so that this effect may be due to overlapping periods of education or training over two waves of the panel survey, in some cases.

Receipt of two social welfare payments, unemployment compensation and lone parent's allowance also increase the probability of entering education/training or an employment scheme in the subsequent year. The positive effects of these two social welfare categories is likely to be due to the targeting of active labour market programmes on particular social welfare categories (recipients of unemployment compensation and lone parent's allowances). Therefore the training and education opportunities open to this group are greater. This benefit effect does not emerge for the transition to employment; only those receiving sickness- or disability-related payment are found to have a distinctive (lower) transition rate into employment.

5.5. Conclusion

This chapter has examined the factors associated with women accomplishing transitions from home duties to paid work. We find that a number of factors are systematically related to the probability of making a transition to work. First, job-seeking is very important: women who were actively seeking work at any point in time are substantially more likely to be working at the time of the subsequent interview. With regard to personal characteristics, age and education are important. Women aged

45 years or older are less likely than those under 25 to make the transition to work, independent of the time spent out of the labour market. However, there is no difference in transition probabilities between women in the 25–44 year age-group and younger women. Education is also important, although when we take account of labour market variables, only those who have attended third-level education have a higher propensity than those at other education levels to enter employment. The higher rates of transition among those with third-level education is likely to reflect two processes: first, an ability to secure a worthwhile wage, and second, possession of marketable skills.

We found little evidence to suggest that either marital status or the labour market situation of a woman's partner influence the probability of entering employment from home duties. Neither did provision of care for an elderly or other relative in the home. We did, however, find that women with younger children, under the age of 5, are less likely than those with either older children, or no children at all, to make the transition to work. While some of this effect will be due to women choosing not to return before their children start school, since a significant proportion of women with children under 5 were seeking work (Chapter 2), this result is also likely to reflect the significant barrier posed by the lack of affordable, good quality childcare (especially for those who cannot command a high wage).

The duration of time spent in home duties is also important, and we found that those who had been out of the labour force for two or more years were less likely to make a transition to enter employment than those who had worked in the previous two years. We also found a reduction of this negative effect among those who had been out of the labour force for 15–20 years, a pattern which we suggest may be related to a return to work after the completion of child-rearing. Recent participation in education or training did not influence the probability of entering employment. In general, receipt of social welfare income maintenance payments does not influence the transition to work, with the single exception of sickness- and disability-related payments, which reduced the probability of entering employment. Women living in urban areas are more likely to move from home duties to employment than their rural counterparts, an effect which is presumably related to the greater work opportunities available in urban areas. This finding is consistent with the views expressed by rural women in our focus group, who mentioned, in particular, the lack of part-time opportunities available locally.

Finally, when we extend the analysis to include transitions to education, training or state-sponsored temporary employment schemes, we find that those who were seeking work in any year are more likely to be in education, training or an employment scheme than in home duties the following year. It is worrying that those with fewest qualifications are least likely to enter education, training or employment schemes, given that these are the group most likely to need such support. This may reflect the formal education requirements that operate for many education programmes and training schemes (see Chapter 4). Access to basic courses and further progression to specific skills training are an important policy issue for this group of women.

Lack of recent work experience also appeared to be a barrier to re-entering training, education or employment schemes; this may again reflect lack of eligibility to employment schemes in particular, or a lack of interest, knowledge or confidence to make such a transition after a long period outside the labour market. Age also influenced the transition to education, training or employment schemes: older women are less likely to make this transition. Receipt of social welfare payments also influenced the transition to education, training or employment schemes. Two social welfare payment categories increased the probability of this transition — unemployment compensation and lone parent's allowance. This is probably due to targeting of active labour market programmes and eligibility rules regarding access to such programmes in operation during the 1994–1999 period covered by the data.

Chapter 6

QUALITY OF EMPLOYMENT

In the previous chapter, we did not differentiate between the jobs obtained by women returners; all transitions into employment were seen as "successful". However, there is substantial evidence that the jobs women enter following a period full-time in the home are often low-paid, part-time, do not fully utilise their skills and are often lower level positions than the women previously occupied. For example, Chaney's early study of returners in Northern England found that the majority of women returned to unskilled cleaning and food preparation jobs (Chaney, 1981). More recent longitudinal studies of women's careers in the UK (McRae, 1993; Joshi and Hinde, 1993) demonstrated that when women return to work from a period of full-time childcare, they often experience occupational downgrading, reduced earnings and fewer promotion opportunities. Studies of women's and men's wages in the Irish labour market have also shown that there is a high earnings penalty for time spent out of the labour market (Barrett et al., 2000). Therefore in this chapter we investigate the types of jobs found by women returners in terms of occupations entered, hours of work, pay, satisfaction, and skill-usage. Using the qualitative data, we also explore whether these jobs met the expectations women have in returning to work.

6.1 Focus Group Interviews

There is a widespread perception among the service providers we spoke to that women are often returning to low-paid jobs. The FÁS representative mentioned that low pay was a significant problem for women following the RTW programmes, and advocated greater progression onto other training courses to improve their pay prospects. Others felt that returners sometimes made a trade-off between pay and flexibility:

> A lot of women returners . . . are coming back quicker now than they used to so it's not teenage children but it's still young children who are at home. And it seems a lot of them are maybe trading off flexible working hours against good pay. (INOU representative)

Institutional factors were also seen as playing a role in reinforcing low pay. The existence of payment systems that could not reward new entrants with experience *outside* paid employment (described in Chapter 4), means that returners often start at the bottom of the pay scale. Elements of the social welfare system were also seen to play a role in making low-paid employment attractive on occasion: lone mothers returning to work may have an incentive to keep their pay below the earnings disregard in order to retain the security of the full OPFP benefit.

> Low-paid jobs become attractive and low pay in itself is attractive because if you are moving from the main payment to lone parents into work there is a very low ceiling, in Celtic tiger terms, it is £115.38, which is a very low ceiling before you start losing your benefit. (Lone Parent Group representative)

Similarly, a lone parent in the trainees' group opted for low-paid informal employment to avoid losing her rent allowance:

> Now I had to give up the cleaning because I'd lose my rent subsidy. So I do it during the day — and I get paid for that — and I would like to be in a situation where I could get some help with my rent if I went back out to work. Because I know that I could probably earn a lot of money. Like these girls have been trained, I can't see why I can't be trained, but I am held back 'cause I keep saying, well, I have to keep a roof over my head. So I'm

in that catch and I want to get out of that catch. (Course participant)

Others also mentioned wanting to work cash-in-hand, which restricted the type of work that they could opt for; these were also women in receipt of social welfare benefits.

The women who had already returned to work rarely mentioned pay levels while discussing their current jobs; instead they focused on the hours of work and the tasks they were involved in. This partly reflected women's priorities: first and foremost they had to find a job that allowed them to combine employment and family responsibilities; only then could they consider other aspects of employment (see Chapter 4).

> If I get more respite care or residential care for my daughter, maybe I could work part-time, I would like that. But it would have to be locally. (Rural woman, working full-time in the home)

However, low levels of pay were clearly a factor keeping women out of employment, especially those who would have to pay for childcare (see Chapter 4).

Work Conditions and Work Satisfaction

In Chapter 4, it was reported that some service providers, especially trainers, believed that returners may have unrealistic expectations about work practices and working conditions. Whether expectations were unrealistic or not, some of the returners were disappointed with their work situation:

> But even for someone who was out of the workforce for so long I was absolutely horrified. Like basic stuff . . . basic things like the post doesn't go out and basic stuff. . . . I mean, why should we be worried about it for £6 an hour, you know. But I find it frustrating and also it's not a very busy switchboard so you're told to read a book, which I find absolutely incredible that you go to work and you're told to read a book. And literally, that is what I'm told to

do and I can't cope with that — I wanted to go back to
work. So I, I'm very frustrated at the moment. (Course
participant)

Some service providers also raised the issue that the support
ends for returners at the workplace door and there is inade-
quate support once they get back in a job. For example, it was
outlined that those re-entering nursing were coming into a
stressful environment with labour shortages and that this could
be difficult to cope with:

> We're talking about trying to get people back in at a time
> when everything is very, very stressed, there seems to
> be very little recognition given to people for the work
> they have done, there seems to be more pressure piled
> on them and that's a lot of stress if you are just coming
> back in. . . . They may get the training initially but then
> they are expected to function like everyone else. (INO
> representative)

One of the CERT trainees recounted her experience of being
left alone to run a catering outlet in her second week on the job,
without supervision or back-up. She left the job as a result and
went back to cleaning:

> They asked me to come back and I said, "no". Well I
> thought I was doing brilliant but I wasn't ready to take
> over the whole coffee dock and train somebody in in the
> second week, and so I've been doing cleaning in the
> evenings — two hours in the evening, you know — just to
> get out of the house. (Course participant)

The issue of follow-up support was also raised in relation to on-
the-job training, and opportunities for promotion/progression.
Participants in the groups identified both institutional barriers
and low expectations of the women themselves:

> Quite a number [of returners] come in part-time in quite
> a lot of places. . . . And when they do get them in, I think

there may be an issue with career progression, particularly for older women. I think most employers do provide initial training, in terms of how to use a PC, how to send out an e-mail, but I'm not sure what space there is, if someone comes in and they're 45 or 50, how much progression do they make? Well, I think in terms of developing a career for them. . . . I'm not sure that there are many supports there. (Chambers of Commerce representative)

I think a lot of women who are returners don't actively think about that [progression] themselves at all, it is a little job, it's a little extra money into the household, or that kind of a thing, but they're not thinking about it as something they get any personal satisfaction from. (INOU representative)

The tension between wanting a satisfying job, or one that just brings in some money without adding stress to the difficult task of combining work and family, was also present in the attitudes of women outside the labour market:

I'd want to go back to something that I *really* wanted to do now. I think that my priorities have changed completely. I don't want to go back to any old job that is boring 9–5, 'cos, that's, you know, I *could* be at home with the kids — why go out and do something that I don't want to do? (Working full-time in the home)

I always think that if I did go back, I'd actually be the opposite. I'd like something that was, like, working in Dunnes Stores so I wouldn't be awake at night and worrying about it, that I could just go in and work in a bar or a restaurant and leave at the end of the evening and forget about it. (Working full-time in the home)

This was also echoed by one of the rural group of women:

Working part-time, I never want to go back to full-time employment, not with four children. You just want quality of life. Working full-time and overtime, I've done that

now, and I don't want to go back to that. I want a job that I
am not stressed out at. (Rural woman, full-time in the
home)

In the following section, we look at the jobs obtained by women
returners using data from the Living in Ireland surveys. This allows us to see whether the perceptions of service providers and
the experiences of the women we spoke to in depth are borne
out at a broader, more representative basis.

6.2 Survey Results

In this section, we use Living in Ireland survey data to examine
the type of jobs that women re-enter. We look at four different
aspects of employment: occupation, hours, pay and satisfaction.
We include women who made the transition from home duties
to employment between any of the two survey years.

Looking first at occupation, rather than applying a socio-
economic or class framework, in which the women are likely to
cluster in very few categories, we examined the occupational
codes individually and picked out the most common occupational groups. These are outlined in Table 6.1. The majority of
women returners are found to enter personal service jobs. The
proportion entering such jobs rose from just under 50 per cent
in 1995 to 64 per cent in 1999. Within this grouping the most
common occupations are shop assistant (which accounts for 13
per cent of jobs on average over the five years), waitressing
and other catering work (12 per cent on average), domestic
work (11 per cent) and cleaning (10 per cent). These jobs tend
to be unskilled and low paid and, for many, represent a con-
tinuation of the unpaid work they have been doing in the home.
Occupations classified under "other service" include hairdress-
ing and hospital orderlies/attendants.

Table 6.1: Jobs Entered by Women Who Moved from Home Duties to Employment (%)

	1995	1996	1997	1998	1999	Mean[1]
Manufact — machine operator/assembly	14.2	20.4	8.3	22.0	5.2	14.0
Clerical — typing, book-keeping	15.5	6.6	14.3	7.5	10.4	10.9
Personal Service Work	49.4	56.3	58.7	54.6	64.4	56.7
Shop assistant	*6.9*	*16.2*	*15.9*	*14.8*	*13.3*	*13.4*
Waitress, bar work, cook	*4.5*	*15.0*	*3.0*	*8.1*	*18.1*	*9.7*
Domestic — housekeeping, cleaning, childcare	*17.4*	*11.9*	*11.5*	*13.1*	*6.8*	*12.2*
Cleaners	*11.6*	*9.1*	*16.5*	*5.1*	*13.3*	*11.1*
Other service workers	*8.9*	*4.0*	*11.7*	*13.6*	*12.8*	*10.2*
Profess/manager/tech	9.3	9.1	5.8	10.5	10.3	9.0
Other	0.0	0.8	1.6	2.0	3.1	1.9
Self-employed/farmer	11.7	6.8	11.4	3.2	6.6	7.9
Total	100.0	100.0	100.0	100.0	100.0	100.4
Unweighted N	*108*	*92*	*108*	*70*	*76*	

[1] Mean of five annual percentage figures, i.e. all years given equal weight.

On average, 11 per cent of the women who found jobs entered clerical occupations such as typing, receptionist and computer operator. In general, this group is likely to enjoy better conditions than those in the service occupations outlined above. On average, 14 per cent of the women entered manufacturing jobs. These were overwhelmingly production or machine operation jobs; for example, packing, canning, electrical equipment assembly, and sewing/machinists.

Only around 9 per cent of the returners found employment in professional, managerial and technical jobs each year. The most common professional jobs entered were teaching, nursing and other health associate professionals (e.g. physiotherapy).

Technical occupations recorded include insurance broker, commercial traveller and bus driver. The low proportion of women entering these higher-level jobs may arise because women in these occupations are less likely to interrupt their careers. The issue of whether women returners are maintaining their previous position or experiencing downgrading is examined below when we compare current job to last occupation.

Between three and eight per cent of the returners entered self-employment each year. The occupations of the self-employed returners were not all that different to those of employees. For example, of the 18 women who (re)entered self-employment between 1994 and 1995, four were in childcare occupations, two were hairdressers, two were shop proprietors and three were involved in farming. Entry into farming must be interpreted cautiously, as these are more likely to involve a re-definition of status rather than a change in activity (i.e. these may not really be returns because it is likely that the women were already working on a family farm).

If we compare the distribution of current occupations of returners to the last occupation held by the same women, we can see that there has been a shift. Table 6.2 presents the previous occupations of women who made the transition from home duties to work between 1994–95 and 1998–99. It should be remembered that for around half of these women, this information relates to a job they left ten or more years previously. The table excludes the small minority who had never worked before and a few cases where information was missing.

The first change to be noted is that fewer of the women were re-employed in manufacturing jobs, which reflects general changes in the structure of employment in Ireland over the time period considered. An even larger decline can be observed in the proportion of women in clerical jobs. For example, a quarter of the women who returned to work in 1999 had previously been in a clerical occupation, but only 10 per cent of the group found clerical jobs when they returned to work. This does not reflect any reduction in the proportion of clerical jobs in the economy in general, and may reflect a process of occupational downgrading if women can no longer secure one of these white-collar jobs when they return to work.

Table 6.2: Last Occupation of Women Returners (%)

	Returned 1994–95		Returned 1998–99	
	Last	*Current*	*Last*	*Current*
Manufact — machine operator/ assembly	19.9	14.2	15.4	5.2
Clerical — typing, bookkeeping	27.9	15.5	24.3	10.4
Personal Service Work — total	35.3	49.4	49.3	64.4
Shop assistant	*10.4*	*6.9*	*9.7*	*13.3*
Waitress, bar work, cook	*11.9*	*4.5*	*16.2*	*18.1*
Domestic — housekeeping, cleaning, childcare.	*1.7*	*17.4*	*8.7*	*6.8*
Cleaners	*7.2*	*11.6*	*11.1*	*13.3*
Other service workers	*4.1*	*8.9*	*3.6*	*12.8*
Profess/manager/tech	11.8	9.3	10.9	10.3
Other	0.4	0.0	0.0	3.1
Self employed/farmer	4.8	11.7	0.0	6.6
Total	100.0	100.0	100.0	100.0
Unweighted N	*95*	*108*	*63*	*76*

The occupations that show the largest increase are personal service occupations. We saw that 49 per cent of 1995 returners were in such jobs but only 35 per cent had been in this occupational group in their last job. This is due to many women taking up cleaning and domestic jobs when they had not been in such jobs before. In 1999, these jobs again show an increase compared to past occupations, but it is "other service" occupations that increase most. This increase in the most elementary occupations (cleaning, domestic work) suggests that occupational downgrading has taken place at a general level. Further detail about the exact nature of the jobs women have within different categories would be needed to make this judgement in individual cases.

The high take-up of personal service jobs compared to the jobs women have occupied in the past may arise because these occupations are more likely to offer the flexible conditions or simply shorter hours that women returners often require (see above). In the following table, we will see the extraordinarily high incidence of part-time working among returners. Service-sector jobs are also likely to be more locally based and so fulfil a need for conveniently located employment.

The proportion entering professional/managerial/technical jobs is almost equal to the proportion of women who left such jobs, which suggests that those with higher initial skills or qualifications are better able to sustain their overall occupational position over time. However, much more detailed information about the level of current and last jobs within this broad category and other conditions of employment would be needed to confirm this.

Finally, we can see that a higher proportion of returners enter self-employment than we would predict on the basis of their previous occupations. Only 5 per cent of 1995 returners and none of the 1999 returners were self-employed in their last occupation. Self-employment may also allow returners greater flexibility to organise their own hours and perhaps work from home; these were factors seen as desirable by focus group members when discussing future employment.

Working Hours

Table 6.3 shows that the great majority of women returners take up part-time work. On average, 71 per cent enter part-time employment each year, although this varied from 60 per cent in 1996 to 88 per cent in 1999. Moreover, the hours worked on these jobs were generally quite low; for example, in 1995, 22 per cent of returners were working less than 15 hours a week, and the average numbers of hours worked was 24 hours per week. These low hours partly reflect the fact that we are using an ILO definition of employment which counts any work for pay or profit of one or more hours per week.

The prevalence of part-time working among women returners is much higher than for female workers in general (see Table 6.4). It remains to be seen whether returners chose these hours to fit in with continuing care/domestic responsibilities, as a half way step back into employment, or if they cannot find full-time work. This question is investigated in Table 6.5 below.

Table 6.3: Full and Part-time Work among Women Returners (%)

	1995	1996	1997	1998	1999	Mean[1]
Part-time[2]	70.4	59.5	74.0	62.3	88.7	71.0
Full-time	29.6	40.5	26.0	37.7	11.3	29.0
	100.0	100.0	100.0	100.0	100	100.0
Mean hrs per week	*24.2*	*25.3*	*22.4*	*22.5*	*17.5*	
Unweighted N	*107*	*92*	*106*	*70*	*76*	

[1] Mean of five annual percentage figures, i.e. all years given equal weight.

[2] Part-time= less than 30 hours per week.

Table 6.4: Full and Part-time Work among All Women in the Workforce (%)

	1995	1996	1997	1998	1999	Mean[1]
Part-time[2]	31.2	27.6	31.2	29.2	33.8	30.6
Full-time	68.8	72.4	68.8	70.8	66.2	69.4
	100.0	100.0	100.0	100.0	100.0	100.0
Unweighted N	*1,501*	*1,342*	*1,337*	*1,266*	*1,093*	

[1] Mean of five annual percentage figures, i.e. all years given equal weight.

[2] Part-time= less than 30 hours per week.

It is interesting to note that the proportion of respondents who are working part-time because they could not find a full-time job declined dramatically over the period of the study. Of those who made the transition into work between 1994 and 1995, just under a quarter said they were working part-time because they could not find full-time employment. However, in 1999 when 88 per cent of returners were working part-time, only 1 per cent said they could not find full-time work. This decline occurred at a time of growing employment opportunities, which suggests that returners had a greater chance of securing their preferred hours. Nevertheless, the main reason for working part-time throughout the period was childcare and domestic responsibilities; given the lack of alternatives, especially in terms of affordable childcare, these part-time hours cannot be seen as purely voluntary.

Table 6.5: Reasons for Working Part-time among Female Returners (%)

	1995	1996	1997	1998	1999	Mean[1]
Hswrk/Childcare	32.5	41.3	38.8	57.9	72.8	48.7
Cannot find full-time job	23.6	33.3	23.7	6.2	1.0	17.6
Do not want full-time job/more hrs	21.1	10.1	34.3	34.1	18.3	23.6
Consider this full-time	9.6	2.1	0.5	0.6	1.8	2.9
Other	13.2	13.2	2.8	1.2	6.2	7.3
	100.0	100.0	100	100	100.1	100.0
Unweighted N	*66*	*49*	*55*	*38*	*76*	

[1] Mean of five annual percentage figures, i.e. all years given equal weight.

Earnings

The mean gross hourly wage of women returners was £4.27 (€5.42) for those who made the transition to work between 1994 and 1995 and £5.36 (€6.81) for those who returned to work between the 1998 and 1999 surveys (see Table 6.6). Given that the average wage can be pulled upwards by a few high earners, we also report the median hourly wage, which cuts the earnings distribution at the half-way point. The median hourly wage for returners was £4.07 (€5.17) in 1995 and £5.00 (€6.35) in 1999.[1]

Table 6.6: Mean and Median Gross Hourly Earnings

	Mean Hourly Wage		Median Hourly Wage	
	Returners	*All Women*	*Returners*	*All Women*
1995	£4.27	£7.04	£4.06	£5.46
1996	£4.39	£7.51	£3.87	£5.92
1997	£4.92	£7.39	£4.02	£5.94
1998	£4.54	£8.08	£3.60	£6.23
1999	£5.36	£7.51	£5.00	£6.20

* excludes self employed

The average hourly wages of returners are significantly lower than the average for all women in each of the years studied. The difference ranged from £3.54 (€4.49) in 1998 to £2.51 (€3.19) in 1999; however, it should be remembered that there is a margin of error attached to these estimates. Similarly, there was a wide gap in the median hourly earnings of returners and that for all female employees of between £1.20 (€1.52) and £2.63 (€3.34).

It is interesting to examine the proportion of returners earning less than the national minimum wage (NMW) rate of £4.40 (€5.59). The NMW was not introduced until April 2000, after the period of our study. Nevertheless, we have data relating to late 1999, which is close to this point. The data from 1999 show that 30.4 per cent of returners were earning less than £4.40. Nolan and McCormick (1999) estimated that a minimum wage set at £4.40 would affect 17 per cent of female employees and 11 per cent of male employees. The current results suggest that

---

[1] The earnings figures are based on gross payments before any deductions have been made for tax, social insurance, pension etc. Information was collected about the last pay packet, the period this covered and the usual hours worked per week. These three pieces of information were used to calculate the hourly wage. The earnings figures exclude those who are self-employed.

returners make up many of the women affected by the minimum wage. However, given that the qualitative evidence suggests that returners sometimes favour work that is cash-in-hand, it is unlikely that everyone will benefit from the NMW.

These findings confirm the impression of service providers that many returners are moving into low-paid employment. Previous research has shown that years of work experience and years out of the labour market have a strong effect on earnings (Barrett et al., 2000), which is likely to influence the results found here. Nevertheless, as the focus group discussants made clear, women may also gain valuable experience outside paid employment, which is often not reflected in their pay and employment position. Further research is needed to establish whether returners are earning less than others with similar education, skills levels and experience.

Satisfaction with Employment

Those in jobs of 15 hours or more per week were asked a series of questions about whether they were using their skills on the job and on their satisfaction with different elements of employment. The findings of previous research, which suggest that returners are often underemployed in the sense that their skills are under-utilised, are supported by our results. Around half of returners in every year feel that they have skills or qualifications to do a more demanding job than the one they are doing (Table 6.7). However, this is also true of other female workers. When we examine the responses to this question by all women in employment (Table 6.8) they are similar to those of returners. This underemployment represents both a loss to the economy and a loss to the women themselves, who are likely to be under-rewarded because of this gap between their skills and their job.

Table 6.7: Returners — Have the Skills/Qualifications to do More Demanding Job (%)

	1995	1996	1997	1998	1999	Mean[1]
Yes	41.9	55.9	48.8	56.0	42.5	49.0
No	58.1	44.1	51.2	44.0	57.5	51.0
	100.0	100.0	100.0	100.0	100	100.0
Weighted N	*74*	*65*	*55*	*46*	*48*	

* Excludes women working less than 15 hours a week

[1] Mean of five annual percentage figures, i.e. all years given equal weight.

Table 6.8: All Women in Paid Work — Skills/Qualifications to do a More Demanding Job (%)

	1995	1996	1997	1998	1999	Mean[1]
Yes	54.3	50.2	54.4	50.8	51.5	52.2
No	45.7	49.8	45.6	49.2	48.5	47.8
	100.0	100.0	100.0	100.0	100.0	100.0
Weighted N	*1,326*	*1,248*	*1,164*	*1,142*	*1,032*	

* Excludes women working less than 15 hours a week

[1] Mean of five annual percentage figures, i.e. all years given equal weight.

Job Satisfaction

Respondents were asked to express their satisfaction with seven elements of their jobs and working conditions: earnings, job security, type of work, number of hours, working times (i.e. daytime, night-time, shifts, etc.), conditions in their place of work and distance to job/commuting. Interviewees were asked to rank their satisfaction on a scale from one to six, where one is "not satisfied at all" and six is "fully satisfied". In Table 6.9, we present returners' responses in two years — 1995, because this is the year in which we have the highest number of transitions (into jobs of 15 hours or more) and 1998, to give a more recent picture (we did not choose 1999 because that year was untyp-

ical in the proportion of women returning to part-time jobs —
see above).

Returners are found to be most satisfied with the working
times, conditions, distance to work and, in 1998, the number of
hours worked. Lower mean satisfaction scores were recorded
in relation to earnings, job security and type of work.

Table 6.9: Job Satisfaction among Women in Paid Work
(higher scores indicate greater satisfaction)

	1995		1998	
	Returners	*Not Return in Last Year*	*Returners*	*Not Return in Last Year*
Satisfied with earnings	3.8	4.0	4.1	4.0
Satisfied with job security	**3.9**	**4.6**	4.3	4.7
Satisfied with type of work	**4.4**	**4.8**	4.5	4.9
Satisfied with n hours worked	4.5	4.7	5.0	4.8
Satisfied with working times	4.9	5.0	5.3	5.0
Satisfied with conditions	5.0	4.8	4.8	4.9
Satisfied with distance/commute	4.9	5.0	**5.4**	**4.9**

Bold figures indicate a statistically significant difference between the two
groups (p < .05)

There is little difference between the mean satisfaction scores
of returners and employed women who have not returned to
work in the previous year. In 1995, returners are found to be
less satisfied than non-returners with two dimensions of employment: security and type of work. Returners are likely to be
less secure because by definition they have been in their current jobs for less than 12 months; furthermore, some of the oc-

cupations entered, e.g. cleaning, domestic work, waitressing, have a significant element of casual employment. The unskilled nature of many of the jobs entered by returners is also likely to explain their lower satisfaction with the type of work performed. In 1998, differences on these two dimensions were in the same direction but did not reach the level of statistical significance.[2] In this later year, returners were found to be more satisfied with the distance to work than other female workers.

These results reinforce the qualitative findings that convenience factors, such as hours and location, may take precedence over intrinsic and extrinsic rewards for some returners.

Conclusions

The analysis that we have carried out on the Living in Ireland survey data provides, for the first time, detailed and representative information on the types of jobs that women returners enter. The evidence is not overly encouraging. The majority of returners are taking up jobs that are low skilled and low status and offer little opportunity for advancement. Returners are concentrated in personal service occupations, which often replicate the unpaid work they perform in the home, with cleaning, childcare, catering and other domestic work all featuring prominently. The return jobs are much more concentrated in the personal service sector than the previous jobs of returners. This increased concentration is particularly noticeable in cleaning and domestic occupations and suggests that there has been a general occupational downgrading. Personal service jobs are perhaps more likely to provide the flexible working hours, convenient location and opportunity for informal work that the women in our focus groups mentioned.

The desire for flexible hours was reflected in the very high proportion of women who return part-time (on average 71 per

---

[2] The difference in satisfaction with type of work almost reached statistical significance ($p = .08$).

cent over the five years) and by the significant number who work less than 15 hours a week. Short hours indicate returners' continuing responsibility for childcare and domestic work; just under half of those working part-time said that it was because of these responsibilities.

However, these "preferences" have implications for the quality of employment found by returners. Both the quantitative and the qualitative research suggests that returners are often forced to make a trade-off between rewarding employment, in both a monetary and intrinsic sense, and work that offers suitable hours or a convenient location. Returners are found to have significantly lower hourly earnings than other women. Further investigation is required to identify the sources of this difference. They are also found to be more dissatisfied with the security of their jobs and the type of work they do compared to other women; however, their satisfaction on other job dimensions are similar. It appears that, faced with limited options, returners are grateful for jobs that meet their minimum requirements and do not express dissatisfaction even when their objective conditions are below average.

The evidence that half of returners feel they could do more demanding jobs suggests that returners have the potential to improve their situation and for employers to make greater use of their resources. This reinforces the calls from many of the service providers for support, training and progression to continue for returners once they enter jobs.

Chapter 7

CONCLUSIONS AND IMPLICATIONS FOR POLICY

The focus of this study has been to explore the experiences of women in full-time home duties wishing to return to employment, education or training, to identify the barriers to their participation and the supports needed to assist their re-entry. The study was carried out using two complementary methodologies. Firstly, qualitative interviews/focus groups were conducted with women outside the labour market, with those who had taken part in education/training courses and with relevant service providers. Secondly, data from the Living in Ireland (LII) survey were used to analyse the factors associated with making the transition from home duties into employment, education and training, and to profile the characteristics of the jobs obtained by women returners. For the purposes of the analysis, returners were defined as women who had spent a period full-time in the home and subsequently entered employment, education, training or government employment schemes.

Here we summarise the main issues highlighted by the study and draw out the policy implications of our findings. The findings are grouped under four main headings: childcare, information, education and training provision, and employment issues.

7.1 Childcare

The issue of childcare arose in both the qualitative and quantitative elements of the study. The lack of childcare provision was identified by the service providers and women interviewed as one of the most significant barriers to women returning to education, training and the labour market. The survey analysis showed that, among women in home duties, those with children under five were significantly less likely to be seeking employment than other groups. Furthermore, analyses of women's labour market experiences over time showed that (controlling for job search and other factors) women with children in this age group were much less likely to make the transition from working full-time in the home into paid employment.

However, childcare concerns were not confined to those with preschool children. The absence of after-school care was a problem for women with school-going children and meant that many were confined to part-time jobs, with consequent implications for the quality of their employment (see below). Older women's opportunities to engage in education, training or employment were also constrained because, as grandparents, they were often required to fill gaps in affordable childcare provision.

While current childcare difficulties represented a barrier for some of those with young children, the longer-term impact of past caring activities was also evident in the strong negative effect of time out of the labour market on the likelihood of returning to employment. The pay penalties attached to spending time in full-time caring have also been highlighted in other studies (Barrett et al., 2000; O'Connell and Gash, 2001).

The past three years have seen an increased policy concern with the expansion of childcare provision. However, such developments are starting from an extremely low base, given that Ireland has one of the lowest levels of publicly funded childcare in the EU, and the cost of private childcare as a proportion of average earnings in Ireland is amongst the highest in the EU (National Childcare Strategy, 1999). The National Development

Plan (1999) allocated £250 million (€317.43 million) for expenditure on childcare over a six-year period.[1] The objectives stated include increasing the number of childcare places and facilities, improving the quality of childcare provision, and providing childcare for the purpose of making education, training and labour market opportunities more accessible, and to "address the needs of men and women generally in reconciling their childcare needs with their participation in the labour force".

The target for the programme is to create 28,208 new places by 2006. Funding approved to the end of 2001 is expected to create 12,278 places, 7,575 (61 per cent) in community-based facilities and 4,703 (39 per cent) in private facilities; however, no information is available of the number of new places created to date. It is still too early to evaluate the long-term impact of these measures on the availability of affordable, quality childcare. Our survey data on the transition from full-time home duties to work pre-date these measures. The data from the focus groups was collected in the middle of year two of the programme. Given that there was a significant under-spend on the childcare measure of the NDP in year one,[2] it is unlikely that many of our respondents would have benefited from this programme by the summer of 2001.

The Goodbody report on childcare (1998) predicts that, at a minimum, the demand for childcare places will increase by 40,000 by 2011, and by another 14,000 if the ratio of women working part-time to full-time decreases. These predictions are

---

[1] An additional £26.5 million (€33.65 million) was allocated to childcare in October 2000 by an anti-inflation package agreed by the government and social partners. A further £67.5 million (€85.71 million) was transferred to Department of Justice, Equality and Law Reform in 2001 from the Departments of Education and Science, and Social, Community and Family Affairs to consolidate childcare funding in one department (Childcare Directorate, D/JELR).

[2] In the BMW region, expenditure in 2000 was estimated to be 8.7 per cent of the target (BMW Operational Programme, 2001). The Southern and Eastern region progress report for 2000 also notes that expenditure on childcare facilities was lagging behind planned spending "due to capacity constraints in construction and the establishment process".

consistent with recent results from the QNHS, which show that the proportion of mothers in employment increased very substantially between mid-1998 and mid-2001. The employment rate of married mothers rose from 43.6 per cent to 49.5 per cent in just three years (CSO, November 2001). On the basis of these predictions, if the NDP targets are reached, the number of new places should just keep pace with new demand to 2006;[3] however, further significant funding post-2006 will be needed to meet continuing increases in demand. Since a considerable proportion of the new provision is expected to be in the private sector, affordability of childcare is likely to continue to be an issue for returners in the future.

Childcare for Participants in Education and Training

Discussions with the service providers revealed that, at present, childcare provision for participants on education and training courses is variable across centres, institutions and types of courses. Where childcare was directly provided by educators and trainers (e.g. by universities, CERT, and community education groups), the number of places was limited and often could not meet the demand among course participants. Community education providers felt that they did not have the financial resources to meet this need.

Childcare allowances of £50 (€63.49) per week are available for the sub-group of women returners eligible to participate on VTOS courses. Since the completion of the fieldwork for this study, a £50 (€63.49) childcare allowance has been introduced for FÁS trainees (in September 2001). However, concerns have been raised that the pay-the-provider system (i.e. payment is made to the carer rather than the trainee) used will exclude many of those relying on informal types of childcare because the providers will have to declare earnings (NESF, 2001). Infor-

---

[3] This assumes that the rate of take-up of childcare among the employed and mothers in home duties remains the same as in 1996. Goodbody's estimate that if the rate doubles for those in home duties, demand would rise by another 43,000 (1998, p. 23).

mal care currently accounts for the bulk of the childcare sector in Ireland[4] although it is not clear what proportion of childminders pay tax or are liable for taxation. Therefore we recommend that the operation of this allowance should be monitored, and if take-up levels are low, alternative arrangements, such as direct payment to the trainee, should be considered.

It is also important that the value of the allowance keeps pace with rising childcare costs.[5] Unfortunately, there are no up-to-date national figures on childcare costs in Ireland. An ESRI survey on childcare carried out in 1997 suggested that average weekly childcare costs ranged from £56 (€71.10) to £71 (€90.15) depending on the type of care (National Childcare Strategy, 1999). However, crèche costs in Dublin are now in the region of £100 (€127) to £130 (€165) per week, while Childminding Ireland, a national association for childminders, recommends a fee of £3.15 (€4.00) per hour, which works out at £126 (€160) for a 40-hour week. A recent ICTU survey of six member unions found that the mean hourly cost of childcare was £3.76 (€4.77), rising to £4.10 (€5.21) in the formal sector (2002, pp. 11–12). This suggests that there is a significant gap between current allowances and costs in the regulated childcare sector.

The results of this research suggest that childcare remains a barrier for women returning to employment, education and training, and reinforces the recommendations of the *Working Group on Women's Access to Labour Market Opportunities* (DSCFA, 2000), henceforth referred to as the Women's Access Report. While there was a consensus among interviewees that childcare provision needs to be good quality, affordable and flexible in terms of the hours available, the preferred form of

---

[4] The childcare survey included in the Commission on the Family report found that the majority of mothers in paid employment used informal types of childcare (Williams and Collins, 1998). Similarly, a survey of ICTU members found that 43 per cent of respondents used informally paid childcare, 22 per cent used unpaid childcare and 35 per cent used formally paid services (ICTU, 2002).

[5] This is one of the recommendations of the NESF report on lone parents.

childcare provision varied among both mothers and service providers. It is outside the scope of this study to assess the most appropriate means of meeting this need for returners or to evaluate the effectiveness of recent measures. However, it is crucial that the take-up of childcare allowances and the supply of childcare places by the state, employers and private providers are monitored. To evaluate the effectiveness of policy interventions, it is imperative that the deficit of information on the current supply and use of childcare is met so that a "before and after" picture can be established.

7.2 Information

The qualitative interviews with women and voluntary agencies revealed that access to information is a critical issue in facilitating the successful return to education, training and employment. Women outside the labour market lacked information on the type of courses and schemes available, the eligibility requirements for these courses, the nature of application procedures and course content. Similarly, they tended to lack knowledge about the kind of job opportunities available in the current labour market. It should be noted that the majority of the women who participated in our focus groups had been in contact with voluntary or state agencies;[6] therefore, the findings on lack of access to information are likely to be amplified among the general population of women returners. Both the Women's Access Report (DFSCA, 2000) and the report by Cousins (1996) highlighted the lack of clear, comprehensive, up-to-date listings on course availability and eligibility, and this continues to be an issue.[7] Indeed, it was often difficult for the

---

[6] Even those who had not made such contacts might be more connected or proactive than women who would not choose to participate in focus groups.

[7] One example of out-of-date information is the Department of Education website, which in December 2001 mentions that 10 per cent of VTOS places are available to certain categories of welfare recipients not on the Live Register, even though the 10 per cent quota was removed in 1998.

research team members to locate written information on these topics.

Information on Course Content

Knowledge about course content was often sparse, even among those who had enrolled on programmes. Some participants reported that the content was not what they had expected or been led to believe. In some cases, the actual content surpassed expectations. However, in general, availability of accurate information on course content is important for course completion (Action Group on Access to Third Level Education, 2001).

Information on Eligibility

There is continuing confusion among women returners about their entitlement to access state training and employment services. While FÁS maintain that there are no formal live register requirements for training programmes, this has not filtered through to potential returners. This confusion may persist because access to FÁS employment schemes (e.g. CE, Jobstart, Workplace, Back to Work Allowance)[8] and to other state educational programmes (VTOS) are still restricted to those on the Live Register and other specific welfare groups. Given that CE is the largest programme run by FÁS, it is perhaps unsurprising that the eligibility requirements for that programme colour public perceptions regarding access to other FÁS services. Confusion may also continue because returners are not given the same priority in the allocation of training places as the registered unemployed if demand exceeds the number of places available (DSCFA, 2000).

We recommend that further action be taken to get the message through to potential participants that they are entitled and welcome to take part in all FÁS training courses. At a minimum,

---

[8] See Working Group Report on Access (2000, p. 40) for a comprehensive listing of programmes that restrict access to those on the live register or in other welfare categories.

all publicly funded agencies providing adult education and training should issue a clear statement regarding eligibility and access to all of their programmes and schemes. A wider publicity campaign targeted at women in the home, providing information on general eligibility and the broad types of courses available, would help to fill many of the information gaps and would fit in with commitments contained within the employment action plans to assist women to return to work.

Dissemination of Information

Our qualitative research suggests that informal networks were the most common source of information for women who have returned to education or training, with many women hearing of the course or scheme through friends and neighbours. Service providers also valued these informal channels because past or current participants could provide reassurance as well as information, effectively acting as positive role models. This method of sharing information appeared particularly important to community education groups. The use of informal networks to communicate information could be further supported through outreach programmes, and by ensuring that course participants have ready access to information about the range of services and courses available. Some members of the third-level education sector have been developing an outreach model of information dissemination, as has the City of Dublin Vocational Education Committee.

The disadvantage of "word-of-mouth" methods of dissemination is that they exclude those who are unconnected to existing social networks; for example, new residents to an area. Several novel methods of targeting this group were mentioned by interviewees, including the use of public health nurses, notices in GP surgeries or local post offices.

Local media also represented an important information source. Childcare and transport factors meant that many returners would only consider local employment, training or education opportunities. Given this geographical restriction, it is likely that local media can supply more relevant information to this target group. National campaigns may be more useful for publicising general eligibility or recruitment drives in particular sectors, rather than providing information on specific courses. The successful literacy campaign, "Read Write Now", which was publicised on national radio and television, represents a useful model on how these media might be utilised.

There are a number of existing information services that interviewees identified as being very useful sources of information about access and eligibility, such as the Citizens' Information Centres. However, knowledge about this service among returners and potential returners was varied, as is the geographical spread of these agencies. Efforts to promote greater public awareness of existing resources, where they exist, would be more cost-effective than re-inventing or reproducing services.

Data Resources

Information is key for policy-makers as well as returners themselves. There is currently a deficit of information on how many participants in education and training programmes are returners. At present, the only returners that can be identified in the FÁS and CERT figures are women who participate in the Return to Work schemes. Women who enter other courses from full-time home duties cannot be identified. Therefore it is essential that these agencies collect information on the prior status of participants in all state-sponsored training and education programmes. Information on the length of time women have spent outside the labour market is also relevant to assessing the training needs of this group, as a parallel to information collected on unemployment duration. Without such information, it will be impossible to measure improvements in access for returners or to evaluate the effectiveness of different policy interventions in this area.

As mentioned at the outset of this study, women's labour market situation might better be conceived of as a continuum rather than a set of discrete states because of the degree of fluidity in women's labour market attachment. From this perspective, it is important that data sources contain information on women's future employment plans in addition to information about their current position. Our analysis of the LII data showed that information on seeking employment was a very strong predictor of future employment among returners. Such data could be supplemented with information about plans to enter education/training and future labour market preferences.

7.3 Education and Training Provision

A number of policy issues were highlighted in relation to education and training provision for women returners; these included access to courses and schemes, the extent of part-time provision, the content of education/training courses and progression routes out of education/training.

Access to Courses and Schemes

In many cases, membership of a particular category (such as the long-term unemployed or qualified adults) operates as a gateway to participation in training and employment schemes. For example, women returners *per se* do not have access to the Vocational Training and Opportunities Scheme (VTOS) or to the Community Employment Scheme. Even where live register status is not a formal access condition, it is often used as a filter when demand for places exceeds existing supply (DFSCA, 2000).

The importance of not distinguishing between different groups of women on the basis of age, family status and benefit status in access to courses was strongly emphasised by the women interviewed for the study. The immediate implementation of the recommendation in the Women's Access Report (DFSCA, 2000) for extending VTOS eligibility to returners would be an initial step in this direction. However, this should not be seen as the end point. Adopting a lifelong learning perspective would involve a more fundamental shift to basing access to all courses and programmes on the education/training needs of participants rather than on their own or their spouse's benefit status.[9]

The quantitative analysis found that the actual level of return to education/training is higher among women with Leaving Certificate or third-level qualifications (see Chapter 5). Interviewees considered that access to education/training should not be predicated on prior success in the initial educational system. Currently, the mechanism for adult entry to third-level courses varies across institutions (Action Group on Access to Third-level Education, 2001) and the extent to which prior education is taken into account may vary across course types. We support the call from the Action Group on Access to Third-level Education that a transparent procedure be introduced for assessing applications and that greater recognition should be given to prior skills and experiences in determining access to third-level courses.

Part-time Provision of Education and Training

The extent to which education/training is provided on a part-time basis varies considerably across providers, types of courses and geographical areas. Both key informants and women returners felt that the lack of part-time provision acts as an obstacle to participation by women returners. Greater flexibility has been introduced through the provision of part-time community-based courses by FÁS and CERT. However, this provision is limited to "return to work" courses while other schemes, including specific skills training, remain full-time in nature. As with training, formal return to education (such as VTOS) and third-level courses tend to be full-time in nature.

---

[9] NESF (2000) recommend that women returners should be designated as a priority group within FÁS employment services and training provision. This would remove an important barrier for returners but retains a "category-based" rather than "needs-based" model of provision.

The Back to Education Initiative promises to co-ordinate existing provision (including VTOS among other courses) and to ex-
pand the number of part-time places available on these courses
by 20,000 (Department of Education and Science, 2000). However, the BEI is yet to be implemented and the initiative limits
access to a subset of women returners (those dependent on social welfare payments or FIS) rather than applying to the group
as a whole.

Community education provides a flexible model of educational provision in that courses tend to be run during primary
school hours. However, the lack of accreditation of these
courses may act as an impediment to progression into further
education, training or employment among participants, and
thus it cannot be seen as a general solution to the lack of part-
time provision in other areas (see below). It is recommended
that the provision of education and training courses by statutory
agencies be made more flexible in terms of the hours during
which courses are run.[10] Flexible hours should be made available not only in courses specifically targeted at women returners but also in specific skills courses, which may be
subsequently accessed by this group. Furthermore, due to the
geographical variation in relation to both part-time and full-
time education/training provision, it is recommended that specific measures are introduced to cater for those in more geographically isolated areas.

The Content of Education/Training Courses

It was felt that existing provision was not necessarily responsive
to the full range of needs and capacities found among women
returners. We suggest that course design should draw from the
experience of community education in developing more appropriate and flexible content in courses and schemes. Currently many of the participants on statutory training courses

---

[10] This issue has also been emphasised by NESF in relation to provision for
returners and for lone parents (NESF, 2000, 2001).

have a relatively low level of initial education. Women with somewhat higher educational qualifications may also benefit from the confidence-building and support provided by education/training provision in making the transition back into the labour market but may not require the basic training element in the Return to Work Programmes. This points to a potential gap in provision for better-educated women returners.

The confidence-building and personal development aspects of education/training courses were highly valued by course participants. The women interviewed felt that the courses they had taken gave them greater self-confidence and the ability to think differently about their lives. It is recommended that modules relating to personal development and effectiveness be incorporated into all courses (potentially) catering for women returners.

Progression Routes Out of Education/Training

Participation in education/training does not necessarily result in re-integration into the labour market (see Chapter 4) or in a progression from pre-employment/foundation to employment-related courses. In some cases, particularly for participants in community education, this may reflect the fact that social contact or personal development represented women's primary motivation for participating in a course. In other cases, however, lack of progression may reflect barriers experienced by the women concerned. It was felt that appropriate guidance and support services should be made available to ensure progression from education/training courses into further training or employment for those women who so desire it. The pilot Adult Educational Guidance Initiative may provide a model in this respect.

The lack of a coherent qualification framework also acts as a potential obstacle to further progression. In particular, the lack of accreditation for community education courses may cause difficulties in this respect. It is recommended that this issue of accrediting prior learning should be addressed by the National

Qualifications Authority of Ireland (see DSCFA, 2000; WERRC, 2001).

7.4 Employment of Returners

A number of policy issues were highlighted in terms of the successful transition to paid employment; these included access to employment, employment conditions, pay levels and progression opportunities.

Access to Employment

There was a consensus among interviewees that the skills developed by women who have been working full-time at home are inadequately recognised in terms of access to employment. Further attention should be given to ways of recognising these skills in recruitment procedures, for example by altering application forms to allow space for skills acquired outside paid employment and experiences of non-formal learning.

Employment Conditions

The survey results contained in this study provide for the first time representative information on the type of employment entered by women returners. Many of the returners entered low-skilled and low-status jobs that offered little opportunity for advancement, such as cleaning and other domestic work, waitressing, and shop work. The jobs they took on re-entering work were disproportionately concentrated in the personal service sector compared with their last jobs, and the pattern suggests that a general occupational downgrading had taken place. This conclusion is supported by the high proportion of returners in the survey who felt they have the skills to do a more demanding job.

A number of potential reasons for this downgrading emerged from the study. Firstly, the qualitative research suggested that factors such as lack of confidence meant that many returners had quite low aspirations on return to the labour force. The focus groups with course participants suggested that low self-confidence was a problem that could be successfully tackled through personal development in training and education courses. Encouraging women to recognise the skills they have developed in the home is also key to improving women's aspirations (see above).

An additional explanation is that low-level employment was the price returners paid for "family-friendly" employment. The vast majority of returners entered part-time jobs (71 per cent on average), primarily because of family and domestic responsibilities. The qualitative research revealed that these responsibilities also restricted returners to locally based employment. Women themselves recognised that these restrictions on hours and location reduced their potential choices and earning capacity. Women in rural areas felt their employment opportunities were particularly constrained and our quantitative analyses confirmed that those outside the main cities were significantly less likely to return to work, all else being equal.

The concentration of women in personal service occupations is likely to reflect these compromises. The results of the research suggest that opportunities for family-friendly employment are not evenly spread across occupations. Encouraging a wider range of employers to provide more flexible employment options is therefore extremely important for the opportunities facing returners. It was also suggested that employers need to develop more innovative employment practices such as term-time working arrangements to encourage more women back into employment.

Division of Unpaid Work

Equally it should be recognised that opening up opportunities for women to return to work on a more equal basis also requires changes in the gendered division of labour in the home (see Chapter 4). The majority of returners are moving from a traditional household arrangement where they have been full-time homemakers and their husband has been the breadwinner. Entering part-time work avoids challenging this gender order and rarely results in men taking a greater share of caring and domestic work (Layte, 1999). Working with women returners on negotiating these issues with other family members was an element of some education/training courses described by key informants, and is worth further evaluation.

Pay

The pay levels of returners represents another aspect of the trade-off between flexibility and "quality" of employment. Hourly rates of pay among women returners were significantly lower than average female wages in each year analysed and 30 per cent of the group were found to be earning less than £4.40 (€5.59) in late 1999, a few months before the National Minimum Wage was introduced at this level. The results underline the significance of the NMW for the earnings of women returners and the importance of monitoring the gender impact of future changes in the value of the minimum wage.

In this study, we compared returners' hourly earnings to those of other women workers without controlling for differences in education levels and years of experience. Further detailed research on this topic is needed to separate out the effects of these characteristics and factors such as working part-time.

Employment Progression

Interviews with returners and service providers highlighted the need for ongoing support and provision of training opportunities for women who have made the transition into paid employment. Such support was seen as playing an important role in their retention within the labour force. Employers should be encouraged to develop ways of better integrating women returners into the workplace (for example, through induction and mentoring systems) and of providing ongoing access to training in order to facilitate career progression. CERT has piloted a system of mentoring for supervisory trainees which may provide a model for future policy development.[11] Funding has been allocated under the National Development Plan for the purposes of in-company training, which could be used to support ongoing training for returners. However, of the €146 million allocated to this measure, only €1.9 million had been spent in the first year.

The research carried out for this study has focused on the initial job obtained by returners and the first year of this employment. However, little is currently known about the sustainability of these jobs or about the progress the women make in the longer term. Further research is needed to explore whether spending time out of the labour market has long-term consequences for the careers, employment conditions and pay levels of women returners.

---

[11] This information was drawn from the interview with a representative from CERT.

BIBLIOGRAPHY

Action Group on Access to Third Level Education (2001), *Report of the Action Group on Access to Third Level Education*, Stationery Office, Dublin.

Barrett, A., Callan, T., Doris, A., O'Neill, D., Russell, H., Sweetman, O., and McBride, J. (2000), *How Unequal? Men and Women in the Irish Labour Market*, Dublin: Oak Tree Press.

Barrett, A., Whelan, C.T. and Sexton, J.J. (2001), *Employability and its Relevance for the Management of the Live Register*, ESRI Policy Research Series No. 40, Dublin: ESRI.

Chaney, J. (1981), *Social Networks and Job Information: the Situation of Women who Return to Work*, Manchester: Equal Opportunities Commission.

Chisholm, L. (1997), *Getting In, Climbing Up and Breaking Through: Women Returners and Vocational Guidance and Counselling*, Bristol: The Policy Press.

Cousins, M. (1996), *Pathways to Employment for Women Returning to Paid Work*, Dublin: Employment Equality Agency.

CSO (2001), *Quarterly National Household Survey: Household and Family Units Q4 1997 – Q3 2001*, Cork: Central Statistics Office.

Denny, K., Harmon, C. and O'Connell, P.J. (2000), *Investing in People: the Labour Market Impact of Human Resource Interventions Funded under the 1994–1999 Community Support Framework in Ireland*, ESRI Policy Research Series Number 38, Dublin: ESRI.

Department of Education and Science (2000), *Learning for Life: White Paper on Adult Education*, Dublin: Stationery Office.

Department of Finance (2001), *Budget 2001*, Dublin: Stationery Office.

Department of Finance (2000), *Budget 2000*, Dublin: Stationery Office.

Department of Social, Community and Family Affairs (2000), *Report of the Working Group on Women's Access to Labour Market Opportunities*, Dublin: Stationery Office.

Fahey, T. and Russell, H. (2001), *Older People's Preferences for Employment and Retirement in Ireland*, National Council on Ageing and Older People, Report No. 67.

Fahey, T., Russell, H., and Smyth, E. (2000), "Gender Equality, Fertility Decline and Labour Market Patterns among Women in Ireland", in *Bust to Boom? The Irish Experience of Growth and Inequality*, B. Nolan, P.J. O'Connell, and C.T. Whelan (eds.), Dublin: Institute of Public Administration.

Goodbody Economic Consultants (1998), "The Economics of Childcare in Ireland", Dublin: Goodbody.

Higher Education Equality Unit (1999), "Who Cares in the Campus? Childcare in Higher Education Institutions in Ireland", Cork: UCC.

ICTU (2002), *Survey of Childcare Practices: Summary Report*, Dublin: ICTU.

Joshi, H. and Hinde, P.R.A. (1993), "Employment after Childbearing in Post-war Britain: Cohort-Study Evidence on Contrasts within and across Generations", *European Sociological Review*, Vol. 9, No. 3, pp. 203–227.

Lyons, M. (2000), "Mothers Returning to the Irish Labour Market — the Role of Employment and Training Schemes", PhD. Thesis, Queens University Belfast.

Martin, J. and Roberts, C. (1984), *Women and Employment: A Lifetime Perspective*, London: Department of Employment/OPCS.

McRae, S. (1993), "Returning to Work after Childbirth: Opportunities and Inequalities", *European Sociological Review*, Vol. 9, No. 2, pp. 125–138.

Morgan, D.L. (1996), "Focus Groups", *Annual Review of Sociology*, 22: 129–152.

Mulvey, C. (1995), *Bridging the Gap*, Dublin: Clondalkin Women's Network.

National Childcare Strategy (1999), *Report of the Partnership 2000 Expert Working Group on Childcare*, Dublin: Stationery Office.

National Economic and Social Forum (2000), *Alleviating Labour Shortages*, Forum Report No. 19, Dublin: NESF.

National Economic and Social Forum (2001), *Lone Parents*, Forum Report No. 20, Dublin: NESF.

Nolan, B. and McCormick, B. (1999), *The Numbers Affected by the Minimum Wage*, Dublin: Stationery Office.

O'Connell, P.J. (2000), "The dynamics of the Irish labour market in comparative perspective", in *Bust to Boom? The Irish Experience of Growth and Inequality*, B. Nolan, P.J. O'Connell, and C.T. Whelan (eds.), Dublin: IPA, pp. 58–89.

O'Connell, P.J. and Gash, V. (2001), "The Effects of Working Time, Segmentation and Labour Market Mobility on Wages and Pensions in Ireland", ESRI: Working Paper No. 140.

O'Connell, P.J. and McGinnity, F. (1997), *Working Schemes? Active Labour Market Policy in Ireland*, Aldershot: Ashgate.

O'Connell, P.J., McGinnity, F., and Russell, H. (forthcoming), "Working Time Flexibility in Ireland," in *Working Time Flexibility in Europe*, J. O'Reilly (ed.), London: Edward Elgar.

Russell, H. (1996), "Women's Experience of Unemployment: A Study of British Women in the 1980s", D.Phil thesis, University of Oxford.

Russell, H. (2000), "Frustrated Housewives or Unemployed Workers? The Case of Domestic Returners", in *Women and the City: Visibility and Voice in Urban Space*, J. Darke et al. (eds.), Hampshire: Palgrave.

Russell, H. and Corcoran, M.P. (2000), "The Experience of those Claiming the One-parent Family Payment", in *Review of the One-Parent Family Payment*, Department of Social Community and Family Affairs (ed.), Dublin: Stationery Office.

Russell, H. and O'Connell, P.J. (2001). "Getting a Job in Europe: The Transition from Unemployment to Work among Young People in Nine European Countries", *Work, Employment and Society*, Vol. 15, No. 1, pp. 1–24.

WERRC (2001), *At the Forefront: The Role of Women's Community Education in Combating Poverty and Disadvantage in the Republic of Ireland*, Dublin: WERRC/Aontas.

Williams, J. and Collins, C. (1998), "Childcare Arrangements in Ireland — A Report to the Commission on the Family", in *Strengthening Families for Life*, final report of the Commission on the Family.